W9-BKK-352

SUPERVISING STAFF

RIVERSIDE PUBLIC LIBRARY
3 1403 00230 9481

3/10/06

A How-To-Do-It Manual for Librarians

Marcia Trotta

Riverside Public Library
One Burling Road
Riverside, Illinois 60546

HOW-TO-DO-IT MANUALS
FOR LIBRARIANS

NUMBER 141

NEAL-SCHUMAN PUBLISHERS, INC.
New York   London

Published by Neal-Schuman Publishers, Inc.
100 William Street, Suite 2004
New York, NY 10038

Copyright © 2006 by Neal-Schuman Publishers, Inc.

All rights reserved. Reproduction of this book, in whole or in part, without
written permission of the publisher is prohibited.

Printed and bound in the United States of America.

The paper used in this publication meets the minimum requirements of American National Standard for Information Sciences—Permanence of Paper for
Printed Library Materials. ANSI Z39.48-1992.

Library of Congress Cataloging-in-Publication Data

Trotta, Marcia.
    Supervising staff : a how-to-do-it manual for librarians / Marcia Trotta.
       p. cm. — (How-to-do-it manuals for librarians ; no. 141)
    Includes bibliographical references and index.
    ISBN 1-55570-524-3 (alk. paper)
    1. Library personnel management. 2. Library personnel management
—United States. 3. Supervision of employees.   I. Title. II. Series:
How-to-do-it manuals for libraries ; no. 141.
Z682.T76 2006
023'.9—dc22
                                                        2006026107

THE SUPERVISOR'S RESOURCE GUIDE

GUIDE A: GLOSSARY OF IMPORTANT TERMS IN SUPERVISORY WORK

Abilities
Personal characteristics used in performing jobs

Acting appointment
Temporary assignment of a person to a vacant position in the absence of the person who normally fills that position; must have minimum qualifications and receives additional pay

Action plans
Clearly defined directions; the actions that must be taken to reach goals

Americans with Disabilities Act (ADA)
Legislation that increases access to jobs for persons with disabilities

Apprenticeship (Internship)
System in which individual is given instruction and experience on practical and theoretical aspects of job

Attitude
The embodiment of an individual's overall thought process

Benefits
Rewards employees receive in addition to wages

Board of Directors
Individuals empowered to make policy

Brainstorming
Group members generate a number of ideas as solution to problem

Burnout
Condition that occurs when work is no longer meaningful to a person

Coaching
Experienced managerial process that is responsible for training and development of employees

Code of ethics
Document outlining principles of conduct

Compensatory time
Time that is over the normal working hours

Conflict
Overt behavior resulting from either individual or group needs being perceived as blocked

Control
Process of determining if organizational activities are going according to plan

Culture
Something shared by all the members of a group; it shapes behavior or structure

Decision process
Process that identifies conditions needing a response, developing possible courses of action and selecting the most appropriate one for the problem at hand

Discipline
Action taken against an employee who has violated an organizational rule or whose performance has deteriorated to the point where corrective action is needed

Delegating
Technique that gives employees responsible and challenging work assignments

Employee Assistance Program (EAP)
Program that attempts to help employees with stress, burnout, and other personal problems

Empathy
Personal understanding of people and their life situations

Empowerment
Decentralized management which gives subordinates the authority to make decisions

Ethics
Principles of conduct used in decision-making and overseeing behavior of groups and individuals

Expectations
Realistic goals set between supervisors and employees

Feedback
Flow of information from the receiver to the sender

Flexible schedule
Schedule of work hours or days within a core time of operation

Flow process chart
Outlines tasks as a service progresses through the system

Goals
Performance aims established in organization's plan

Grapevine
Informal channels of communication

Grievance
A claim that there has been a violation or misinterpretation of an agreement

Human relations skills
Understanding people and being able to work with them

Implementation
Putting the strategic plan into action

Innovation
Process of applying new and creative ideas to an operation

Input
Individual contributions to an organization

Interpersonal communication
An interactive process of sending and receiving messages between individuals

Job analysis
Process of determining with observation and study all the information related to a specific job

Job description
Written statement that identifies the tasks, duties, activities, and performance results for a particular job

Leader
One who influences willing followers in setting and achieving objectives

Leadership
The ability to influence people who are willing to follow one's guidance and adhere to one's decisions

Long-range objectives
Go beyond current year; must support and not conflict with the mission

Long-range plans
Usually extend at least three to five years into the future

Management
Form of work that involves coordinating organization's resources toward accomplishing organizational objectives

Measures
Standards by which performance is judged

Mission
Statement that defines the basic purpose of why an organization exists

Motivation
This is what directs human behavior toward particular goals

Needs assessment
Systematic analysis of specific activities that help determine an organization's objectives

Objective
Statement that outlines what we are trying to achieve

On-the-job training
This is when the employee receives direction and is allowed to perform job under a trainer's supervision

Operations management
Application of basic concepts and principles to day-to-day workflow

Organizational morale
The feeling of being accepted by and belonging to a group of employees through common goals, confidence in the goals and mission, and the desire to achieve them.

Overtime
Work that is over 40 hours within a seven-day period is paid at a rate of one and one-half times the hourly rate.

Performance Appraisal
Determining how employees are doing on their job based on expectations and establishing a plan for improvement

Policies
> Broad, general guides to actions

Positive reinforcement
> A technique that lauds correct behavior, leading to more of the same

Procedure
> Series of related steps in logical order that are needed to complete a task

Role
> An organized set of behaviors that are identified with a particular job

Self-motivation
> An individual's commitment to the job combined with personal desire to perform well

Shift differential pay
> A bonus paid for working during less desirable hours; in libraries, employees are often compensated for evening or weekend work by a shorter workweek (for example, work 37 and get paid for 40)

Short-range plans
> Plans usually for one year

Skills
> Special competencies in a particular area, including technical ability and people skills

Solution orientation
> Finding alternate solutions to problems and obstacles

Span of management
> Number of subordinates a manager can effectively manage

Staff functions
> Functions that are necessary for the efficiency and productivity of an organization

Strategy
> Basic steps that need to be taken in order to complete an objective

Task
> A particular activity within a job

Technical skills
> Being able to perform the mechanics of a particular job

Temporary pay
> Usually a bonus that is paid if an employee is working above his or her job classification for a short time without receiving a promotion.

Training
> Acquiring skills or learning concepts to increase employee performance

Vision
> The overall long-term ideal for the organization

Workday
> The number of hours within a 24-hour period; 8 hours is equivalent to full time

Workweek
> The number of days/hours assigned to a staff member

GUIDE B: BIBLIOGRAPHY

Association for Library and Information Science Education. "Educating Library and Information Science Professionals for a New Century: The Kaliper Report." Reston, Va.: Association for Library and Information Science Education, 2000.

Beeker, Loren. *First Time Manager*. New York: Amacom, 1993.

Blanchard, Ken, and Sheldon Bowles. *High Five!* New York: William Morrow, 2001.

Blanchard, Ken, and Don Shula. *The Little Book of Coaching: Motivating People to Be Winners*. New York: Harper Business, 2001.

Brown, W.S. *Thirteen Fatal Errors Managers Make and How You Can Avoid Them*. New York: Berkley Books, 1985.

Buhler, Patricia M. "Managing in the New Millennium." In *Supervision*, vol. 65, issue 2, February 2004.

Fry, Ron. *Manage Your Time*, 2nd edition. Franklin Lakes, N.J.: Career Press, 1994.

Gilly, Jerry, and Nathaniel Boughton. *Stop Managing, Start Coaching!* Boston: McGraw-Hill, 1995

Goad, Tom. *First-Time Trainer: A Step-by-Step Quick Guide for Managers, Supervisors and New Training Professionals*. New York: Amacom, 1997.

Greenwald, Joel. "Six Tips on Supervising the 'Office Family.'" In *Business Journal*, vol. 13, issue 5, p. 26

Hargove, Robert. *Masterful Coaching*. San Francisco: Jossey-Bass, Inc., 1995.

Kroeger, Otto, and Janet M. Thuesen. *Type Talk at Work*. New York: Dell, 1993.

Ladew, Donald. *How to Supervise People*. New York: Career Press, 1998.

Merrill, David, and Roger Reid. *Personal Styles and Effective Performance*. New York: CRC Press, 1999.

Newstrom, John, and Edward Scannell. *The Big Book of Teambuilding Games*. Boston: McGraw-Hill, 1998.

Nolan, Harry. "Crisis Planning Must Include Routine, Extreme." In *Business Insurance*, June 21, 2004, vol. 38, p. 10

Parkinson, Tom. *Listening and Helping In the Workplace: A Guide for Managers, Supervisors and Colleagues Who Need To Use Counseling Skills*. New York: Souvenir Press, 1996.

Pollock, Ted. "Mind Your Own Business." In *Supervision,* Vol. 62, issue 2, February 2001, p. 16.

Robbins, Stephen R. *The Truth about Managing People. . . . And*

Nothing but the Truth. Upper Saddle River, N.J.: Prentice Hall, 2003.

Rue, Leslie, and Lloyd Byars. *Management: Skills and Application,* 10th edition. Boston: McGraw-Hill, 2003.

Stack, Peter. *Confident Leader: A Powerful and Practical Tool Kit for Managers and Supervisors.* New York: Human Resource Development Press, 1996.

Stone, Florence. *Coaching, Counseling & Mentoring: How to Choose and Use the Right Tool to Boost Employee Performance.* New York: Amacom, 1998.

Stone, Florence. *The Essential New Manager's Kit.* New York: American Management Association, 2003.

Stone, Florence. *The Manager's Question and Answer Book.* New York: American Management Association, 2003.

Straub, Joseph. *Rookie Manager.* New York: American Management Association, 2003.

Stringer, Robert. *Leadership and Organizational Climate.* Upper Saddle River, N.J.: Prentice Hall, 2002.

Thiedeman, Sondra. *Making Diversity Work.* New York: Dearborn, 2003.

Thompson, Brad. *The New Manager's Handbook.* New York: Richard Irwin, Inc., 1995.

Trotta, Marcia. *Successful Staff Development.* New York: Neal-Schuman, 1995.

Turner, Ann M. *It Comes With the Territory: Handling Problem Situations in Libraries.* Jefferson, N.C.: McFarland & Co., Inc., 1993.

Urbaniak, Anthony. "Training Employees." In *Supervision,* vol. 65, issue 2, February 2004.

Wade, Jared. "Establishing an EOP (Emergency Operations Plan)." In *Risk Management.* vol. 51, June 2004, p. 48.

Wilson, Jennifer. "Now the disaster's happened, what am I supposed to do?" In *Accounting Today,* vol. 18, June 21, 2004, p. 24.

ASSOCIATIONS

The American Management Association
1601 Broadway
New York, New York 10019

The Center for Coaching and Mentoring:
www.coachingandmentoring.com

Manager's Forum:
www.mamagersforum.com/services/coaching.htm

GUIDE C: THE SUPERVISOR'S BOOKSHELF

CHAPTER 1

Drucker, Peter. *Peter Drucker on the Profession of Management.* Boston: Harvard Business School, 1998.

Rue, Leslie, and Lloyd Byars. *Management Skills and Application, 10th Edition.* New York: McGraw-Hill, 2003.

Solomon, William A. *The New Supervisor's Manual.* New York: Amacom, 1999.

CHAPTER 2

Ladew, Donald. *How to Supervise People: Techniques for Getting Results through Others.* Franklin Lakes, N.J.: Career Press, 1998.

Petzinger, Peter. *The New Pioneers: The Men and Women who are Transforming the Workplace and Marketplace.* New York: Simon and Schuster, 1999.

Trout, Jack. *The Power of Simplicity: A Management Guide for Cutting through the Nonsense and Doing Things Right.* New York: McGraw-Hill, 1999.

CHAPTER 3

Kroeger, Otto, and Janet M. Thuesen. *Type Talk at Work.* New York, Dell, 2005.

Maginn, Michael. *Effective Teamwork.* New York: McGraw-Hill, 1994.

CHAPTER 4

Chandler, Steve and Scott Richardson. *100 Ways to Motivate Others.* Frankin Lakes, N.J.: Career Press, 2004.

Ohles, Judith K., and Julies McDonald. *Training Paraprofessionals for Reference Service: A How-to-Do-It Manual.* New York: Neal-Schuman, 1993.

Trotta, Marcia. *Successful Staff Development: A How-to-Do-It Manual.* New York: Neal-Schuman, 1995.

CHAPTER 5

Ellison, Edna. *Woman to Woman: Preparing Yourself to Mentor.* New York: New Hope, 2005.

Flaherty, James. *Coaching: Evoking Excellence in Others.* New York: Butterworth-Heinemann, 2005.

Green, Thad. *Motivation Management: Fueling Performance by Discovering What People Believe About Themselves and Their Organization.* New York: Davies, Black, 2004.

Mullen, Carol. *Mentorship Primer.* New York: Peter Lang, 2000.

Zachary, Lois. *Creating a Mentoring Culture: An Organization's Guide.* New York: Jossey-Bass, 2005.

CHAPTER 6

American Management Association. *Pressing Problems in Modern Organization (that keep us up at night): transforming agendas for research and practice.* New York: American Management Association, 2000.

Curzon, Susan C. *Managing Change: A How-to-Do-It Manual, revised edition.* New York: Neal-Schuman, 2005.

CHAPTER 7

Evan, G. Edward. *Performance Management and Appraisal: A How-to-Do-It Manual.* New York: Neal-Schuman, 2004.

CHAPTER 8

Bradford, David. *Reinventing Organizational Development: New Approaches to Change.* New York: John Wiley, 2005.

Low, Kathleen. *Recruiting Library Staff: A How-to-Do-It Manual.* New York: Neal-Schuman, 1999

Rubin, Richard E. *Hiring Library Employees: A How-To-Do-It Manual.* New York: Neal-Schuman, 1993.

Rubin, Richard E. *Human Resource Management in Libraries: Theory and Practice.* New York: Neal-Schuman, 1991.

CHAPTER 9

Gordon, Rachel Singer. *The Librarian's Guide to Writing for Publication.* Lanham, Md.: Scarecrow Press, 2004.

Newlen, Robert. *The Complete Job Handbook for Librarians and Information Professionals.* New York: Neal-Schuman, 2006.

Nesbitt, Sarah, and Rachel Singer Gordon. *The Information Professional's Guide to Career Development Online.* Medford. N.J.: Information Today, Inc., 2002.

Pantry, Sheila, and Peter Griffiths. *Your Essential Guide to Career Success.* London: Facet Publishing, 2003.

INDEX

CONTENTS

LIST OF FIGURES

PREFACE

A common misconception about librarians is that they work only with things—books, computers, media, software. But those of you who have actually worked in a library know that the majority of your time is spent working with people—both your users and your co-workers. And sometimes the greatest challenge is getting those co-workers to work more productively.

Supervising Staff: A How-To-Do-It Manual for Librarians is a resource for professionals, new and seasoned alike, who want to become better leaders and managers of library workers. While there is no single, step-by-step formula that will help you become a better supervisor, there are proven strategies that can help. This guide looks at the various responsibilities of a library supervisor and provides the best methods for improving your performance in each area.

Being a good supervisor has a lot to do with actions. It requires knowing when and how to act. Some days may require hands-on training with your team; other days may demand that you step back and delegate responsibilities. There are also new responsibilities—budgeting, performance evaluations, and facilities maintenance—that you may have to familiarize yourself with.

Being a good supervisor is also about relationships. Your co-workers may be very eager to work with you. They may also be suspect, challenging your authority and decisions. You may find yourself struggling to set a positive tone among the coworkers, orienting new employees and keeping veteran employees happy.

Finally, being a good supervisor requires that you continue to develop professionally. Those who selected you for this position felt that you were ready for the added responsibility—and they are likely still looking for you to grow and develop. You have to be progressive, learn new things, and keep current. After all, you want the best from your people and you can't have them expect anything less from you.

Some of the advice in *Supervising Staff* may seem eerily familiar. Perhaps you have experienced it firsthand—many of us have had the luxury of being supervised by talented leaders. One of the great secrets of being a successful supervisor is learning from your own experience of being supervised. Successful managers take the time to think about what they have liked and disliked from their previous experiences. I encourage you to read this manual with the same sense of reflection and piece together a supervisory strategy that works for you.

ORGANIZATION

Chapter 1, "Understanding the Supervisor's Role," looks at the differences between the three basic responsibilities—leadership, management, and supervision— you have as a manager and shows how each plays a part in your new role. It looks at the new responsibility you have to your workers and the new challenge of being accountable for their performance. It challenges you to stay true to the qualities and qualifications that brought you to this stage of your career and not give in to the pressures or misconceptions of your title.

Chapter 2, "Mastering Basic Supervision Tools," looks at some of the new tasks you will likely be assigned—planning, organizing, directing, staffing—and how these fit into library work. You will find valuable information on verbal, written, and nonverbal communication. There is also careful guidance for taking on new tasks, something that will be part of your day-to-day experience as a supervisor.

Chapter 3, "Creating and Running Work Teams," will help you create a comfortable, productive work environment for you and your staff. People don't automatically like each other, and things don't just happen. Effective workplaces require teamwork and proper facilitation. This chapter looks at how to organize, direct, and assess teams. You will find checklists and exercises for managing your team.

Chapter 4, "Directing Ongoing Staff Training," tackles one of the most important functions of a supervisor: how to take employees from orientation to mastery of tasks and responsibilities. There is guidance for determining needs, setting goals, and conducting training.

Chapter 5, "Mentoring and Coaching Staff," looks at how the supervisor can inspire his or her workforce. This section will help you learn to motivate your staff, set an example, and promote continuous improvement.

Chapter 6, "Implementing Change and Managing Crisis," helps with both the progress you plan for and the setbacks you never see coming. As a supervisor, you will be able to implement change, but you will also be responsible for helping your staff adapt and thrive in the new environment. Unfortunately, as supervisor, you will likely be the first person to learn about a crisis—and your staff will look to you as a model for reacting. This chapter helps you develop a plan for change and crisis and shares strategies for lessening the impact of these changes and crises on both you and your staff.

Chapter 7, "Using Performance Appraisals Effectively," introduces one of the least popular parts—both for you and your subordinates—of supervision. Performance evaluations, however, are one of the most beneficial tools in your arsenal. They will help you reward, improve, and organize your staff's service. This chapter features several example evaluation forms and tips for scheduling, completing, and delivering your appraisals.

Chapter 8, "Hiring and Retaining a Diverse Workforce," speaks to the staffing responsibilities of the supervisor. In this chapter you will find guidance for developing a personnel policy, taking disciplinary action, handling complaints, and working with union employees. This chapter is filled with sample forms, policies, and worksheets.

Chapter 9, "Taking Charge of Your Career," brings the focus back to you. It outlines the duties and objectives of a manager, recaps some valuable information, and provides exercises and checklists for continuing to learn and grow.

Finally, "The Supervisor's Resource Guide," presents a glossary of important terms, a bibliography, and recommended reading with "The Supervisor's Bookshelf."

You are encouraged to remember the phrase "adapt to your own situation" as you read. The information provided is often generalized in order to accommodate the varying sizes and types of libraries and departments you may find yourself running. *Supervising Staff* is most effective when its guidance is taken and applied to your own unique situations, with special attention to your own unique needs and conditions.

Libraries are labor-intensive organizations. Our staff, more than our collection, is our greatest resource. Effective supervision—"people management"—is central to the library's ability to offer services to its community. As a supervisor you have been given a great challenge and a great opportunity.

ACKNOWLEDGMENTS

I would like to thank Carmine Trotta for his constant patience in allowing me to bounce ideas off him and my editor, Michael Kelley, for his vision with this book.

For my colleagues throughout the library world: Happy supervising!

1 UNDERSTANDING THE SUPERVISOR'S ROLE

ASSUMING THE RESPONSIBILITY

Culture shock hits everyone in charge of supervising staff. As "just an employee," your job was to do your one job well. The shock comes from knowing that now your job relies on your ability to make others do their job well. If this is your first move into supervising, you probably feel both a little excited *and* a little anxious about your new responsibilities. If you have worked as a supervisor for some time and want to become better at the job, there is always something new to learn. In my experience, I have found that I learn the most by networking and sharing with colleagues. I hope that you think of me as a colleague and benefit from the some of the things that I have learned through trial and error. No matter how long you've been a supervisor, you never completely eliminate being a little panic-stricken with the realization that perhaps you may be judged on how well your subordinates perform. What can you do to prepare yourself for this? How do you become ready to face any crisis? Remember at some point in time you were hired or promoted to assume this responsibility. Someone saw your ability to visualize and make decisions. You possessed the right qualifications, and senior management both recognized and had confidence in your ability to handle this opportunity. How can you best demonstrate the strengths your boss expects you to display through daily applications? Remember: It is the supervisor who is potentially the most effective person in the organization to influence employee behavior toward their work and toward the library itself. There is no doubt that you now have an awesome responsibility.

Take heart! You are not alone! Every manager has nervous jitters at first. Some who have attained management positions in libraries had formal preparation for the role through their masters degree program; many others have learned the skills on the job. It goes without saying that everyone wants to be effective at overseeing the work of others. People grow only by being challenged, and being a supervisor will help you grow, as well as your helping others develop. You may work in a small or a large li-

1

brary. You may work in a public, academic, or special library. Your goal as a supervisor will be the same, and there is no denying it—it will be a challenge. Your goal is helping the library accomplish its organizational goals through the work of others, not just yourself. It also helps to remember that as a supervisor you are strategically positioned to be the go-between between upper management and front-line employees. You are now in a position to disseminate information in both directions. Clearly, you are in a job that will make a difference!

> **On the Job Q & A**
>
> Q: What will my job as a supervisor be like day by day?
>
> A: Even though you may have a functional specialty (Head of Reference, Children's Services, etc.), in reality, you will spend most of your time talking with employees. This is a good thing, because if you listen, you will learn a lot.

BECOMING A SUCCESSFUL SUPERVISOR

What does it take to be a successful supervisor? What is the difference between management and supervision? Management addresses the mechanics of the position—the process of budgeting, of developing controls, organization, etc. Supervision addresses the interaction with people in order to get a job done. Management can be defined as the form of work that involves coordinating all of an organization's resources in order to accomplish its objectives. In recent years, the field has become more and more complex and challenging. While the basic tenet still holds true, that management is getting work done through others, supervisors in today's workplace have greater visibility and more accountability than ever before. The times and our changing workplaces have put more and more demands on supervisors. Greater commitment, creativity, and flexibility are now necessary. We are often expected to do more with fewer resources. In fact it does not matter if you are new to management, or have been at it a long time; the supervisor's roles and responsibilities do change with the times. Your abilities and the experience that you will develop counts for a lot, but there is always room for improvement. Remember to look at your supervisory position as an opportunity for you to grow professionally. Then the ongoing growth that is expected of you makes more sense.

A few years ago, the American Library Association had a promotional campaign that claimed, "The greatest resource that a library has goes home every night." That is the purpose of this book. Supervision is about managing these very same people. As a supervisor, you may be called upon to be a manager—to oversee the work of others. You may be called upon to be a mediator and to act as an intermediary between upper management and these employees. You will be a mentor, encouraging growth and development, demonstrating your commitment to our professional values and ethics. And you will be asked to be a leader.

EMBRACING CONFLICT

Because of the nature of the work, "managing people," supervisory positions sometimes present enormous potential for conflict between yourself and others. You will find your job to be a balancing act, and often tricky. There are personality clashes, organizational demands and requirements, and the need for you and your employees to conform to the rules and practices of your library. These are aspects of the job that cannot be ignored. Doing so may cause resentment among people, low productivity, and even high turnover of staff. The book is designed to provide you with the information that you need to deal with these situations and to be the best that you can be in your position. As you read it, you will begin to develop confidence in yourself. This alone will help decrease the stress that comes along with the job. As you rush from one-on-one sessions, to meetings, then to the inevitable crisis, you don't want theory. You want practical, hands-on answers to the daily problems that you will undoubtedly face with the cumulative pressures that come with your new job. Many supervisors are frustrated by the wide range of problems that often do occur on a daily basis. However, as the supervisor, you are indeed the person expected to handle them. You are called upon not only to be a leader of those you supervise, but also to follow directives set up by the library director and the Board of Trustees. You need skills that will be helpful to you in your role as intermediary and skills that make you capable of handling those ever-present demands efficiently. After all, the library's goal is service to its patrons, and good service can only happen when there is good productivity and job satisfaction on the part of supervisors and subordinates alike.

SKILLS AND ABILITIES

Effective management is the implementation of a collection of skills that make you stand out as a leader in your organization.

These are clearly defined and have been proven to work. These skills include:

- communications skills, such as constructive feedback, job coaching, or counseling;
- people skills, including understanding workers and working well with them;
- knowledge of conflict resolution techniques crucial to teamwork;
- motivational skills enhancing your leadership role; and
- time management and endurance skills.
- conceptual sills—being able to understand the relationships between each department of the library to each other department and to the whole system.

In addition to these skills, you will be expected to be able to plan, organize, use judgment, and make decisions. And of course, you will utilize your technical abilities, which ensure that you are able to perform the functions of all of the tasks that you supervise, even if you don't perform them on a day-to-day basis. In the long run, being an effective supervisor will reflect itself in the level of cooperation that you receive from your subordinates. Being decisive, communicating competently, and establishing a working rapport among the people you supervise goes a long way in establishing this credibility.

On the Job Q & A
Q: I've heard that the bulk of my job is going to be giving work orders. True?
A: Be aware of quantity and quality. You will spend time directing work, but the most important part of the job is developing relationships with the people you supervise.

LEADERSHIP

While a middle-management supervisor is usually concerned with day-to-day issues, the importance of leadership must also be stressed. Leadership is the ability to sense and identify relevant needs and aspiration among followers. People want to be able to turn and depend on others, both in times of change and in times of organizational stability. Leadership means that you bring about change when change is needed; it also requires you to protect the status quo when that is the solution that is called for. It is the ability to visualize the way things could be if some changes were made.

The leader possesses skills that allow him or her to come to decisions, solutions, and resolutions. Charismatic leaders make their employees feel more self-esteem, more confident, by making them comfortable personally as well as with the situations they may be addressing. They make workers feel more in control in the workplace. Supervisors who assume a wait-and-see attitude for too long a time, who withdraw from an issue or freeze under pressure—especially when the library is under conditions that require action—are shirking their responsibilities. Action or nonaction surrounding a value (i.e., what the expected norm is for comfort in a situation) is what will count when people perceive your leadership skills.

COACHING AND MENTORING

As a supervisor, you will be asked to coach and empower others to use their skills and expertise to produce results. You will also be required to interact with other divisions or departments within the library's structure. Coordination with these various people and the work that they perform often are requisites for effective library services. As an effective leader, you must have the vision to see the value of this process and inspire trust among people, so that the "Is" are put aside for the value of the whole library.

If you exhibit leadership, then employees will develop the confidence that you will act in their best interest. But understand that you must also serve the needs of the group at the same time. They will recognize that you know when to offer criticism and when to praise them. And they will know that, even as a leader, you will sometimes be expected to follow others.

You will demonstrate this leadership ability as you are an advocate for the people you supervise; when you demonstrate that you are fair without playing favorites; when you are able to implement change without chaos; and when you create a workplace that nurtures and expresses pride in jobs well done. An environment of pride generates positive energy in the workplace, encouraging others to offer new ideas rather than resist change. In times of crisis and change, the supervisor demonstrates leadership by maintaining open communications, so that there are fewer surprises. People respect plans and directions if they feel that they are part of the process and are kept informed. People respect hierarchy if it is clear what the hierarchy is. Everyone in the organization must understand who is responsible for making the tough calls, and what is expected of them. This clarity of command is an empowering tool. Employees need "limits" for this reason, and many will tell you that they are glad that you, not they, have to make the decisions! And finally, as a leader you will be called upon to demonstrate courage as you do the right thing and make those tough decisions. Be advised that those people that you supervise will be watching!

Everyone wants to be liked. However, sometimes, when you are trying to accomplish tasks through the work of others, you may have to make difficult decisions that are not popular with your subordinates. It is especially difficult to be in a position of authority over people who were once your peers. Successful supervision starts with learning to manage subordinates, and newcomers often find that their biggest barrier is their own fear about managing those who they supervise. You worry about your own performance, and about being judged on the performance of your subordinates. The most difficult time for any supervisor is when one has to make the transition from being a worker to being a "boss."

Being promoted from within the organization has several advantages. These include a familiarity with the system and how it operates, as well as knowing the strengths and weaknesses of the employees within the department. However, there are also obstacles. Probably the biggest one is that you are now expected to supervise individuals who were your peers and may also be personal friends. It is a balancing act, because you do not want people to feel that you are a snob because you have a new position, and you don't want to alienate anyone by the appearance of showing favoritism because you have friends in the workplace. You must treat everyone fairly, and you cannot let personal feelings, either good or bad, influence job decisions. It is also hard to adjust to not doing the job you once held. You don't want the person who has taken on your old responsibilities to feel that you don't think he or she is capable of doing the job. And yet, you also don't want to been seen as procrastinating on performing in your new role by providing guidance and supervision. You will come to realize that you will now worry about your own performance and also about being judged on the performance of your subordinates. Take heart, because you will grow into the role!

One of the areas that you will be involved with in your supervisory role is in the area of resource allocation. One might think that this responsibility is the director's, but in actuality, all supervisors make decisions—the scheduling of people, the purchasing of materials—that result in the allocation of resources to one use over another. This resource may also be simply what we set out to do ourselves and what tasks that we choose to perform, or it may be based on what we prioritize as work for our employees. These decisions cause results, which then, in turn, define the organization and its impact. The director should and will hold you accountable for your performance in this area.

It is important that you view your supervisory role from your own perspective as a person, so that you are not just mechanically following rules. In the final analysis, being a successful supervisor means that you have been able to adapt your job to your personality rather than changing yourself so that you can meet the demands of the job. That being said, there are some behavioral qualities you can immediately demonstrate which are helpful as you make the transition to the supervisory role. In fact, these are qualities that will create an atmosphere of respect for you. When I asked colleagues about what they felt were the most important attributes for a supervisor to possess, their answers varied but included the following:

- Keeps up to date on all situations that may affect work
- Organizes schedules and assignments effectively and fairly
- Never plays favorites and enforces rules fairly
- Keeps a positive and upbeat attitude
- Asks questions; always knows what is going on
- Projects a professional attitude
- Gives praise, rewards, and compliments for work well done
- Is a visionary, yet realistic; ideas are explored and set out clearly
- Keeps employees informed of library news/issues especially if it will affect them
- Protects staff from interference
- Develops direction; not confused, but clear, crisp, definite, and precise
- Is customer-driven, not self-driven
- Is proactive and aggressive
- Takes time to listen to new ideas
- Sets a good personal example
- Is thorough
- Is honest
- Doesn't talk "up" or "down" to anyone
- Develops priorities and is results oriented; gets things done
- Avoids generalities when performing tasks; is clear about what is needed
- Understands that implementation is the key to achievement
- Provides training opportunities
- Delegates with clear directions and confidence
- Involves others in the decision-making process
- Is observant and identifies problems before they reach crisis

On the Job Q & A

Q: Do I really want to take on the responsibilities of this job? Why would I want to be a supervisor—there seems to be so many things to deal with every day!

A: It may sound a little corny, but the rewards are great! Passing on your skills to others and preparing others to be the library leaders of the future is particularly gratifying.

- Values employees as individuals as well as team members
- Uses new strategies that will make the system more productive and efficient
- Doesn't lose temper when things go wrong
- Doesn't complain and gets on with the job
- Can admit mistakes when things go wrong
- Doesn't misuse authority
- Shows a human side

Developing the qualities within yourself will give you a head start on your new position and in developing credibility with your subordinates. Some other points to remember are:

- Be yourself! Don't take on a new "persona" because you have a new title
- Be decisive. You don't want to appear "wishy-washy" about making decisions; do your thinking privately so that you don't appear to be unsure of yourself
- Keep your cool. Getting angry alienates people
- Always be fair, objective, and focused. It is not to your or the library's benefit to compromise performance standards or bend rules "for old times sake."
- Be firm when necessary. There are times when you will be tested, and although it is nice to be liked, you still have responsibilities to keep.
- Be friendly, yet maintain your composure in difficult circumstances

We have spoken about things that we want a supervisor to do, but it is also important to look at some of the reasons why there are occasions when people do not do well as supervisors. First and foremost of these is when an individual has been forced to take on a supervisory role when he or she really does not want to do it. If this is the case, it is much better to speak up right away and let someone else take on the role, rather than put yourself in the position of performing poorly. Supervisors must be good role models. They must abide by the rules and set a standard for others to follow. Promotion does not make one exempt from an organization's policies and rules! Sometimes supervisors have an inability to delegate properly. This might mean that the supervisor provides incomplete information about the tasks that he or she delegated, or it might mean that the supervisor delegates a responsibility yet continues to perform the job. Supervisors can also set themselves up for failure if they continue to be a "buddy" to some old friends and fail to treat all employees fairly.

On the Job Q & A

Q: I have just been promoted to supervisor and now some of my former co-workers are calling me "boss lady." They say it jokingly, but it bugs me. What, if anything, should I do?

A: The answer to this question really depends on how well you know these co-workers. Can you tell if they are just joking, or perhaps are jealous of your promotion? Even though it may annoy you, I think it is better to overlook and perhaps even ignore the comments. You don't want to be in a position of making a big deal out of nothing. If you are now their supervisor, you will always want to act with restraint and in a professional manner. If they are jealous, your performance is what will help establish your authority. If the teasing continues for a long time, you then may want to answer with a joking, "Who, me?" I have found that this gets people off the topic fast!

The transition from employee to supervisor requires a willingness to reduce the amount of time one spends on professional activities and increases the time spent on managerial activities. It requires trust in the skills of others and planned decisions that facilitate constructive productivity. This process cannot be left to chance, and should be faced honestly and openly. The responsibilities of supervisors are both diverse and difficult. Sometimes it may feel that every decision you make results in someone being unhappy. Our purpose is not to create an environment that is risk-free, but one in which we can get a job done. It is almost a certainty that there will be someone who is not happy with you; it is part of human nature. It is up to each of us to decide if these demands become a source of frustration for us rather than an opportunity for growth. As you will soon learn, the process of self-development for supervisors is never-ending. We must do our best and continue to take advantage of learning opportunities as they become available.

I wish that I had a magic wand that I could wave and make everyone who is reading this a successful supervisor. Unfortunately, there is no simple formula to make you successful as a supervisor. Managing people in pursuit of a common goal will require you to stretch your talents and your patience!

My goal is to offer you realistic advice that will enable you to avoid the pitfalls of the job. Keep these simple thoughts in mind: Remember that the promotion from employee to supervisor does require a transition. Remember that supervision requires more than capability; it requites knowledge, skills, and probably most important of all, attitude. Supervision is a competency that you will develop through a career-long process, not overnight. With this information, I hope to spare you from having to scramble for the information that you need to handle the wide range of difficult situations that I can guarantee will confront you. These are suggestions, and none of the included information is intended to supersede your organization's own policies and regulations. Nor is every organization the same. Take the suggestions and adapt them so that they become tools that are your own. Remember that if we work effectively, we are doing the right thing, and that working efficiently is doing things right. Take a page from David Letterman and consider these top ten concepts:

1. Treat everyone with respect.
2. "Do unto others" . . . learn to see your actions as if you were on the receiving end.
3. Be willing to stand up and fight for "your" people in the way that you want your boss to stand up for you.

4. Keep your employees accurately informed. Communication is the way to instill trust, and it will keep a lid on damaging rumors.
5. Be accessible. Have an open door policy that lets your employees know that you care about them and their concerns.
6. Handle problems promptly. If you don't have the final authority to resolve an issue, make sure that you carry it to those who do.
7. Keep your emotions in check. Control your temper; don't show your impatience and tenseness.
8. Be true to your own ethical standards. Be yourself and not what others think you should be.
9. Don't let work overwhelm you. Take care to enjoy your leisure time, because being relaxed and well rested prepares you for the challenges of the job.
10. Don't neglect your own career goals. Where do you want to be in three or five years? You must give your all to your current job, but failure to challenge yourself with future growth opportunities will stifle your present behavior.

So let's get started and be supervisors! We want our staff to perform to the best of their abilities so that our libraries will be the best that they can be.

2 MASTERING BASIC SUPERVISION TOOLS

Promotion to a supervisory position is usually a pivotal juncture in a person's career. Often, it is both a reward for good performance and a means of directing good talent into the managerial hierarchy. What do new managers find the most challenging? Frequently, the answer to that question is their primary responsibility, being in charge of other people. The purpose of supervision is to assist a less experienced employee increase his or her effectiveness in the delivery of library services. The supervisor's job is to provide support and encouragement to employees, to help them build their skills and competencies, and to oversee their work. To become an excellent supervisor, one must be both technically competent and also have a clear understanding of management and leadership skills. Many of us had no real idea when we started supervisory work about what we had gotten ourselves into. But we learn to juggle diverse responsibilities, untangle a web of relationships, and often deal with conflicting demands.

This chapter is intended to help you figure out what to do and how to act so that you can become a responsible supervisor; it should guide you in decision-making and being accountable for those decisions; and it will provide you with some tools so that you can provide others with opportunity while their efficiency and productivity increases.

UNDERSTANDING LIBRARY MANAGEMENT

An analysis of the management process helps us understand the framework that is in place for the administration of libraries. In order for a library to be successful, I believe that there must be unity of direction—i.e., a clearly stated mission. This is set out by the Board of Trustees and the Director. However, the most successful situations are those in which both staff and community input has been used to set the mission. Most libraries, except the very smallest, are usually divided into departments. These departments encompass the principle of the division of labor. It is through this process that we separate out work that is distinct to a particular function, such as technical services, or children's services.

On the Job Q & A

Q: A longtime employee is obviously disgruntled, but when I ask him directly what's wrong, he says, "It's nothing." Should I respect his privacy and let it pass or should I try another way to draw him out?

A: The answer to this question may vary depending on how well you know the employee. Were you co-workers before you became his supervisor, or is this someone you just met? I would advise you to give the employee a little space. However, I would observe and listen to him carefully (and discreetly) and see if you can determine if he is disgruntled with you, the job, his colleagues, whatever. He may say something to someone else, or you may see tension between him and someone else. There may also be something from his personal life troubling him, and he is just not ready to share it. If he knows that you are concerned, he may come to you on his own. If you see that the person is not doing his job because of this attitude, I would definitely take him aside and ask if there is something bothering him that you can change.

For efficiency and economy, there are some functions that are better organized into a central location. A circulation department responsible for the control of lending all materials within the library is an example of this principle put into action. Specialization naturally develops within the division of work. Another area of management is the concept of authority. In areas when individuals are given a specific responsibility, they should also be given the level of authority necessary to complete the tasks.

Most management textbooks would be in agreement that there are specific management functions that apply across the board to every organization. These are the broad areas that every manager oversees to some degree. They include:

Planning, which is the process of identifying the strategic choices that the library should make. The plans are based on the contribution that the library is prepared to make within the community and its intended impact. Planning is a term that represents an encompassing outline for all of the things that need to be done. Very often the plan will include methods or strategies of accomplishing these items so that the mission can be met. Planning is also an important tool in helping the organization determine its long-term vision. The goals and strategies that are planned must be specific and measurable. They should also be "time bound," so that boundaries for achieving them are established. If an assignment is given to a particular person for one of the specific goals, that person should be given the authority to complete it and a time frame as well as the responsibility for the task.

Organizing is the responsibility of the director. However, in most situations it is achieved with input and assistance from the supervisors. Through this process, jobs, tasks and workflows are identified and assigned. Specialized tasks or procedures may be assigned, and the interaction and interdependence among departments is determined. Through this function, the procedural infrastructure of the library is determined.

Staffing means that supervisors must match the requirements of the job with the knowledge and skills of its staff. This is a never-ending process, since both the job requirements and the people who work for us change. Recruitment, orientation, and ongoing training are important parts of this management function. Performance appraisals which document how people are performing and developing as well as individual goal setting are also part of this charge.

Directing is the area which manages the day-to-day interactions between various people and departments. Organizational ground rules with policies and procedures are necessary for these interactions. Depending on the size of the organization, supervisors, as well as the director, will have to be versed in this management practice. Directing is the continuous task of making decisions and presenting them within policies and instructions to carry out the work.

Control functions are those that help us make sure that the actions we take to perform our jobs are in accordance with accepted policies and standards, and meet the objectives of our strategic plan. These include statistical data, such as "number of items circulated" or "how many reference transactions," as well as others. Controls must be evaluated and interpreted, as they are most often designed to keep the library on course and to ensure that the same controls are placed on everyone equally. Coordinating is the important duty of interrelating the tasks and work of the various units or departments for the overall good. Reporting is the term that is used to refer to the responsibility of the director to keep the Board informed of day-to-day as well as long-term plans. Oftentimes supervisors are asked to prepare a report on the unit they supervise. Reporting requires accountability. In order to be consistent with accountability, there are agreed-upon controls and a process to provide information to a governing authority.

Budgeting is a particular type of control. It is the fiscal planning, accounting, and control of the financial resources that are necessary to run the operation efficiently and effectively. It is predicting what monies will be needed and alternate sources (gifts, grants) to get them if not fully funded by the city, college, etc. Again, this function is usually overseen by the Director. However, supervisors may be required to present budgeting information for the operation of their departments.

Every type of organization has its mission-specific function, and libraries are not any different. School libraries need media specialists on staff; academic libraries may have a greater need than public libraries for subject specialists. The Director has the responsibility, along with the Board of Directors, to evaluate specific staffing needs. However, as a supervisor you may be asked to contribute ideas in this area so that service delivery will be improved. In addition every organization has functional needs, such as marketing, budgeting, development, purchasing, legal, maintenance. These special functions may be handled solely by a director or a specific designee; a variety of "specialists" or contractors may be assigned to accomplish these tasks. However, it is not outside the realm of possibility that as a supervisor you may be assigned to assist with some of these operational duties.

The application of all of these management principles is the basis of having an effective organization. The service that we provide is effective if we can anticipate change and have appropriate responses to user needs designed quickly. Needless to say, we are often judged by our ability to implement these responses to needs at minimal costs.

On the Job Q & A

Q: What do I do if a staff member comes to work dressed inappropriately?

A: I would advise you to take him or her aside privately for an opportunity to speak first. Maybe the reason for wearing jeans on the job that day was that his washer/dryer was broken and he had no other clean clothes. If he says anything, then you should ask in a nonthreatening way why he is dressed out of code. Have a copy of the library's written dress code policy available and remind staff members that they were informed of what was acceptable or not acceptable dress at their orientation session. A word of caution: it is imperative that you follow written policy here. You want to avoid anything that may be interpreted as sexual harassment.

COMMUNICATIONS: THE PRIME MANAGEMENT SKILL

If I had to rank the importance of the skills necessary to be a supervisor, I would say that communications skills, both written and oral, are central to all supervisory positions.

Experts have claimed that 90 percent of all organizational problems stem from ineffective communication. It is no wonder then that every supervisor has a responsibility to keep his or her people informed. Most people want to know what's happening. However, we should be aware that because we are bombarded with so much information, people respond more readily to interesting, relevant, and entertaining messages. People process information in different ways, and different messages work best with particular media types. It is to our advantage to select the most appropriate communications method for a particular situation, but we should avail ourselves of using as many as possible. Surveys, memos, newsletters, brochures, updates, and polls can be delivered in print or electronically. Communications between supervisors and staff can occur at formal meetings, through phone calls or e-mails, and through planning, goal setting, and training and appraisal opportunities. Communications also happen informally, sometimes with a remark made in passing, so we need to be careful about what we say and how we say it. It is important not to overlook the office "grapevine." Gossip on the grapevine might be destructive, and unclear messages may cause problems. However, getting news spread quickly and efficiently can be one of the grapevine's greatest benefits if the supervisor begins the grapevine process with an employee who is a reputable communicator.

There are many good things that happen in organizations that no one hears about. The supervisor has a responsibility to share these items with others. How do you keep good ideas and good news flowing? Internal communications transmit information about achievements and plans; they disseminate creative ideas and practices; communicate cares, concerns, and needs; and transmit organizational standards. The three categories of internal communications are interpersonal, which is most often face-to-face among people; mass communications, which are wide-ranging and often not conveyed in person; and nonverbal, which includes body language and graphic messages.

DEVELOPING COMMUNICATION SKILLS

Good communication skills are essential in effectively supervising others. They will also determine how well staff members work as a team. Positive communication skills will help you every day in your role as a supervisor. Whenever we have the opportunity to communicate with others, there are several things that we can do to make sure that our discussions remain productive and friendly.

In the workplace, there are many different ways that we communicate with each other. We do this orally from casual conversations that we have with one another, through phone calls and voice messages, and through more formal presentations. We communicate through written methods, such as reports, memos, and plans, and more recently through faxed and e-mailed documents. A key point for every supervisor is to assume the responsibility all of the department's communications, whether sent or received. This is because the role of supervisor demands that we understand other people, and if they have not sent us an understandable message, then we have to follow up and see what it is about. Communication is about listening and understanding as well as sending messages.

Some key points that can guide you in the communications process are as follows. First, it is important not to take anything for granted. For example, if you are receiving data or information from someone who has provided incorrect information in the past, or you don't know the source well, it is important to check it yourself. If you have been given instructions or directions from your supervisor, and you feel that you do not completely understand what is expected, you should verify them. It is far better to ask questions or ask for additional explanations than to waste time doing a task incorrectly. It is not a sign of incompetence or disrespect—rather, an effort to be correct. Use this same method with employees. Encourage your employees to follow your example and to question you. Let them know what you expect. They cannot read your mind! Show them, and when appropriate, give them written instructions/directions to follow. When you really

On the Job Q & A

Q: My staff sometimes overlooks messages. Do you have any suggestions for ways to reinforce a message?

A: Training and memos are traditional business practices for this. However, if you want to put a little fun into your reinforcement techniques, try crossword puzzles. These can be made on any subject. You can purchase an inexpensive software program to construct them easily. This gives learning new tasks a refreshing and fun twist.

need a communication to be in writing, make sure that you get it. Oral communications are more personal, but if they go through too many layers of personnel, the message may not be recognizable by the time that it gets to you. (Remember the game of "telephone" we played as children?) A great deal of information can be unintentionally miscommunicated in this way.

Supervisors must develop their listening skills. Make sure that you give employees your complete attention and are not distracted when it is important that you hear a message. Some other ways that communications can be improved are really simple common sense. Your conversations should be clear and concise. If at all possible, put your messages into writing. Clearly written documents will help you control misunderstandings. Be honest. You don't want to put yourself in a situation where you have intentionally given false information, even if the honest information might hurt the person (e.g., there will be layoffs). It is much better to be truthful. If you truly don't know the answer to a question, it is important that you admit this. Then tell the person that you will find out the answer and get back to them. Indeed, do follow up.

There are some questions that you should ask yourself in terms of maintaining a good communications plan as a supervisor. You will want to know who in your department will need input (and what it is) from you before they can do their jobs. You will also need to know who should be sending materials to you so that you can do your job. In our libraries, our departments are interdependent upon one another. Therefore, you will want to ask the very same questions about your communications need with them. Figure 2.1 show some examples of strategies that you can use to improve your abilities as a communicator.

Language and terminology are powerful communications tools. They can communicate expectations. Negative words create a sense of hopelessness and undermine creativity. Positive references can clear the air and are good to promote active involvement and new ideas. Positive ideas can create an open, supportive work environment. Figure 2.2 is a worksheet to help you gauge your communications ability and track improvement.

On the Job Q & A

Q: I'm new on the job. How do I budget?

A: Budgeting refers not only to money but to other resources, such as people. It is good practice to review what has been done previously. You should ask for advice from trusted colleagues or from your supervisor. Use numbers that are realistic based on your research. Be sure that they reflect your operational plans and responsibilities.

Figure 2.1   Sample: Strategies for Two-Way Staff Communications

Interpersonal Strategies

Strategy	Application
Walk around	Do so daily if possible to stay in contact
Staff meetings	Hold on regular basis; follow agenda; feature status reports, opportunity for input, recognition, and major announcements
Word of mouth	Also known as "the grapevine." People pass on information they have heard
Telephone	Person to person
E-mail	Person to Person
Training advisors	Person to person
Job descriptions	Clearly defined functions so people know expectations
Exit interviews	What did you like working here? What would you change?

Mass Communications

Strategy	Application
Display/bulletin board	Highly visible
Memos	Written to appropriate people; good way to update
Newsletters	Widely distributed
Brochures	Widely distributed
Handbooks	Widely distributed
Surveys/focus groups	Ways of getting input

Figure 2.2 Checklist: Improving Supervisory Communications Skills

Start Date:_____

Check the areas of communications where you feel that you may need improvement. Then, develop a plan for improving your communications skills. When you feel that you have improved, indicate that with a date.

Date improved

■ I say "we" or "our library" rather than "they" or "the library" to indicate that I am a part of the organization.

■ I criticize the actions, not the individuals.

■ I don't devalue jobs below mine by saying that someone is "only a. . . ."

■ When someone deserves praise, I give it.

■ I use please and thank you.

■ I speak politely.

■ I avoid the use of vulgarities and offensive expressions.

■ I watch my grammar.

■ I speak with people at a level that makes them comfortable.

■ I don't complain about petty annoyances or argue about trivial matters.

■ I think before I speak.

■ I listen to what others have to say.

On the Job Q & A

Q: I've heard that the correct way to delegate can be summed up as "5 W's and an H." What does this mean?

A: The short answer is: who, what, when, where, why, and how.

NONVERBAL COMMUNICATIONS

When working with people, we also need to remember that we often communicate messages and attitudes through body language. It is important to pay attention to our actions, because they may convey a very different message than the one that is coming out of our mouths. Below are some indicators of behaviors and what interpretation they may have.

Confidence:
- Back stiffened
- Hands on jacket lapels
- Hands behind back

Cooperation
- Open hands
- Sitting on edge of the chair
- Hand-to-face gestures

Openness
- Open hands
- Casual stance

Insecurity
- Hands in pocket
- Chewing pencil
- Wringing hands

Frustration
- "Tsk" sound
- Clenched hands
- Short breaths

Defensiveness
- Arms crossed across chest
- Gestures with fists
- Points with index finger

Suspicion
- Sideways glances
- Moving away

Nervousness
- Fidgeting

- Throat clearing
- Perspiration

PRESENTATIONS AS A COMMUNICATIONS TOOL

On the Job Q & A

Q: What is the "who" of good delegation?

A: "Who" chooses the right person for the task; the assignment must be appropriate for his/her skills and abilities.

The ability to make good presentations is a key in gaining the respect and support of others. Presenting well helps establishes your authority. People will seek you out when you are at ease in front of an audience. Those who supervise you will see you as someone with whom they feel comfortable representing the library. Making presentations is far easier than most people assume. The key to it is thorough preparation. If you know your subject well, you will be able to explain your message clearly. You should have a goal for the presentation. If you know what you want to accomplish, and you gear your presentation toward this end, then you have a much better chance of it succeeding.

It is also imperative that you know your audience, and you should tailor the presentation to that specific audience for the most effectiveness. Using visuals is another way of getting your audience to focus attention on your message. Because people absorb messages in different ways, you will find that you are much more effective if you intersperse words with good graphic representations.

Perception accounts for a great deal of the success of a presentation. Presenters who stand up and use visual aids are perceived as more professional, more persuasive, more credible, and more interesting to listen to. The quality of the presentation *is* the public image of the service that you provide.

Following a few simple rules will be invaluable to you as you prepare presentations. First of all, spend the time to organize your talk. Every good presentation starts with a solid introduction. It should be concise, but it should also tell the audience who you are and why you have been chosen to speak on this topic at this particular time. Generally speaking, the first two minutes of the presentation are the ones that are most listened to by the audience. So, have a solid introduction that is an attention grabber. Present the message with as many support materials as possible to make it credible. These may be examples, comparisons, or quotes. Tailor your presentation to your audience. The only way that you can do this is to learn as much as possible about them

On the Job Q & A

Q: What is the "what" of good delegation?

A: The "what" determines what you will give your staff to do? Paperwork? Technical support? Routine tasks? Tasks that offer learning opportunities? Be clear on the tasks and your expectations on completing them.

before you speak. Always have a conclusion that summarizes the key points that you made. This will leave the audience with the idea that you are a highly effective and well-organized speaker. It is absolutely worth spending some time to develop the critical areas of introduction and conclusion.

Instead of having your presentation written out word for word (believe me, if you do, you will wind up reading it rather than presenting it), have a list of key points in priority order. If you do this in bold, large type, you will be able to keep the organization of your presentation on track without losing eye contact with the audience. Eye contact with the audience is important. It personalizes your message and it seems as if you are speaking directly to people. This makes your message more acceptable.

Use visual aids when they are appropriate. This might be a flip chart or a black or white board, which are effective if you are speaking to a small group of people. A flip chart promotes audience participation, and you are able to write key words in large print for emphasis. This is a factor that triggers the audience into remembering what you are saying. Overhead slides and PowerPoint presentations on a laptop can be used effectively if the images you have prepared look professional. You want to make them clear, in large print, with only a limited amount of information so that they are not distracting. You should also be prepared for things to go wrong—a bulb burns out, the computer won't boot up. Have a backup plan so that you do not become flustered with the inevitable failure of equipment.

Finally, remember that it is not just what you are saying that is important, but how you say it. Your voice carries the message. You should change the pitch with variations and inflections to keep it uplifting, and make sure that your voice is loud enough to be heard without shouting. Again, equipment is important. Does the microphone work? Is it hand-held or a clip-on so that you can move about? Is there static? Do you change your pace of speech and pause when you want to make a point? Are you familiar with all words, phrases, and pronunciations? Stumbling over words does not make a good impression. Practice, practice, practice—that is the best advice that I can give you. Use the following checklist to walk you through the presentation process.

Figure 2.3 Checklist: Tips for Effective Presentations/ Public Speaking

■ Prepare, prepare, prepare. If you know your subject inside and out, you have the best defense against fear.

■ Take the time to visualize how you want your presentation to go before you prepare it.

■ Listen carefully when you are asked questions. Give concise but accurate answers.

■ If you are asked a question and you don't know the answer, tell the truth! Say you don't know, but that you will find out the answer and get back to them.

■ Give yourself a break! Don't be overly critical of yourself. Ask someone you trust to evaluate the presentation, and tell you areas that you need to work on.

■ Talk with your audience, not at them. The information that you are conveying should hold their interest, not yours.

COMMUNICATING THROUGH REPORTS

Sometimes, we don't have the opportunity to present information in person. In these cases, administrators are often called upon to prepare written reports. The best reports are accurate, brief, and clear. They present a summarized overview of the topic in a way that is clear to the reader who may not have firsthand experience with the topic or the issue. The best way to present this information is with precise language that is descriptive of the topic, with backup materials (statistics, references) as appropriate. You may consider providing an "Executive Summary." This is actually an abstract that presents the reader with a compressed version of the report, with emphasis on the most important points. Whenever you prepare a report, you are presenting specific information to a specific audience for a specific purpose. You will want to consider your audience—who are they and exactly what information does your audience need or expect? Of what use will the information be? In what order should it be presented to provide the most help?

Remember your purpose in writing reports. Do you want to inform? Analyze? Persuade? Your writing style and the types and organization of the information that you will need to include will differ based on the purpose.

Figure 2.4   Exercise: Establishing Present Communications Skills Level

Answer the following questions as honestly as you can, and you will get an honest profile of your communications expertise. Then, decide what you are going to do to help improve your communications abilities.

1.   What are your strongest communication skills? What are your weakest communication skills?

2.   How could you be more effective if you improved on the areas where you are weak?

3.   What benefit would gain from improving your communication skills?

4.   Where can you develop the skills that you need?

5.   Have you sent incomplete or incorrect communications? Why?

6.   Have you sent communications to the wrong person?

7.   Were any of your communications delayed or not sent at all?

8.   Were people confused about your message, and did they need more details?

9.   Did anyone report back to you that you communications were unnecessary or irrelevant?

10.   Did you send any communications that contained an overly emotional tone?

There is always room for improvement for all of us. So as you evaluate your answers to these questions, target the one area where you feel that you need the most help and improve it!

The following is a method of improving your communications abilities. There is also a checklist to remind us why it is important that we take the time to be a good communicator.

Figure 2.5   Checklist: Tips for Maintaining Good Communications

- Work together! A good strategy to build and strengthen communications is to avoid letting aggravations accumulate. When frustrations are not dealt with, they can lead to explosions that are not beneficial or pleasant.

- Be honest, but not accusatory. It is easy to blame others when things go wrong. If you show that you are angry, blaming others will only cause retaliation. You don't want to provoke a defensive response, but rather to encourage an open discussion.

- When there is need to address a situation that has gotten out of hand, try to maintain a positive approach. Focus on the concern. Resist the temptation to bring in other issues that have no bearing on the issue at hand. Be willing to compromise. Maintain your self-control and your willingness to be objective and reasonable.

- Maintain eye contact, as it increases credibility.

- Put yourself in the other person's shoes. It is important to keep his perspective in mind, and to value his point of view, even if you don't agree with it. It is your job to listen to and acknowledge other people's concerns and to make an honest attempt to really listen. Then explain your perspective.

- If the communications situation is personal, be sensitive. Your genuine concern is displayed through your voice and actions.

> **Figure 2.6   Checklist: Recognizing the Importance of Communications Skills**
>
> ■ Research shows that over 90 percent of all organizational problems can be traced to ineffective communications.
>
> ■ Most people want to know what is happening in their organization.
>
> ■ The larger the organization, the tougher the communications problems.
>
> ■ People receive thousands of "messages" a day. Only interesting, relevant, or entertaining messages receive full attention.
>
> ■ People learn and process information in different ways— visually or through the audio process, independently, or in groups.
>
> ■ A good supervisor tries to make all communications timely, entertaining and relevant to staff needs and interests
>
> ■ A good supervisor communicates through many different media at different, scheduled intervals
>
> ■ A good supervisor tries to create a positive climate that encourages positive interpersonal communications

COMMUNICATION STYLES HELP MANAGE CONFLICT

Conflict among employees usually follows a series of stages. It is up to you as the supervisor to be alert for this and to use your own skills to handle the problem before it affects the entire department. Using communications effectively is one of the tools that you have at your fingertips to help you deal with these types of situations. In most cases, conflicts escalate with the following steps:

- One person wants something and another disagrees or obstructs progress
- Both parties feel frustrated because they can't do or get what they want
- Frustrations are manifested by blaming each other
- They feel angry and do or say things based on how they each interpret what has happened
- Both parties react, and the conflict escalates

If you recognize conflict, you can take steps to manage it. What you will do will depend upon the severity of the conflict and the urgency with which you must resolve it. Some strategies that may be useful in a conflict situation include:

- Resolving conflict by being dominant or forceful. You would use this strategy when there is an emergency, and quick, decisive action is imperative. If the issue at hand is vital to the library, you may need to take this approach. If people take advantage of others, you must view this as destructive behavior and deal with it forcefully.
- Give in and accommodate. Sometimes it is better to compromise. This will resolve the situation and you will be able to move forward. The need to be right is a human problem; it is always good to allow each person to have some degree of "rightness," even if you have to decide against his or her opinion. This is a good method to use when issues are much more important to others than to the organization.
- Resolve conflicts by using trade-offs or compromise.
- Back up really bad news with specific facts, numbers, and results. This helps to "de-personalize" the situation and can help you maintain control. This is a good way to reach settlement with complex issues, especially when there are conflicting goals. You will sometimes need to use this strategy with your peers.

Good communication is built upon relationships. It is important that supervisors take the time to know the people that they are supervising. It is not a task that is accomplished in a day. Rather, learn a little about the people each day and you will not become overwhelmed.

Some tips for building relationships include:

- Smile
- Be modest

On the Job Q & A

Q: What is the "when" of good delegation?

A: It is important that you know the right time as well as the right person to delegate to. For example, you may choose to use the new assignment as a reward for good performance on another project. However, you may overwhelm the person if he or she has many things to do already. Also, you will want to be clear on the time frame or deadline for when you want the work completed.

- Take a sincere interest in others
- Avoid arguments by keeping conversation on logical levels, for once it drops to emotional levels, arguments will start
- Be positive
- Repeat or paraphrase what you thought you heard, to confirm it
- Ask questions when you really want the answers, offering choices only between acceptable answers
- Know what you want to say—be prepared
- Speak in terms that people can understand
- Be yourself

On the Job Q & A

Q: What is the "where" of good delegation?

A: You will need to decide if you will delegate tasks to an employee publicly. This is a motivator if the person is given some new authority and responsibility and others need to know. In some cases, private assignments are more suitable to the situation.

COMMUNICATING THROUGH EFFECTIVE MEETINGS

As a supervisor, you may find that the number of "meetings" that you are expected to attend has suddenly increased. Meetings are management tools. They may be held to gather information; to approach a problem and find a solution; to share responsibility for necessary actions; to generate new ideas for the library. So, even though meetings can take up a great amount of time, if they are productive, this is time well spent. One criterion that you should employ before you call a meeting as a supervisor is to determine if a meeting is really necessary. There are times when a phone call, memo, or "virtual" meeting are equally effective. Another step is to carefully determine who should be at the meeting. The topic should be relevant to the work of those invited, and they should have something to contribute or they are best left off the meeting list. It is also essential that the purpose of the meeting is clearly understood by all who are attending.

If you come to the decision that a meeting is necessary, time can be saved if some ground rules are established at the outset. Developing an agenda that will lead the group to complete its purpose is important, as is sticking to it. Someone should have the role of taking notes, so that there is a written record of what transpired. Followup reports should be sent to all attending, and to those group members who were unable to attend. These minutes should provide a summary of what occurred, what actions or steps have been determined to reach the goal, and who is responsible for seeing that the action occurs .You should also determine at this time if it is necessary to have additional meetings or whether further business could be conducted in a different way.

It is also important to start and end the meeting on time if you are leading it, and to be prepared to be on time and stay for the entire meeting if you are a participant. Everyone should be respectful of all in attendance. It is never appropriate to participate in side conversations, as they can be exclusive and distracting. While it is important to participate, we should also remember that we should not monopolize conversations. This behavior can be very intimidating to others.

COMPONENT OF GOOD AGENDAS

- Make sure that it clearly communicates the purpose of the meeting and send it out to participants in advance
- Make sure you include the location, time, and date of the meeting
- The agenda should include each item that is to be discussed
- Time limits should be set for each item so that the meeting doesn't run over
- If attendees need to bring any materials with them or need to prepare for the meeting, inform them at this time

CHECKLIST FOR MEETINGS

- Make them brief, focused, and productive
- Make them efficient
- Make them effective
- Have ground rules that all agree to follow
- Establish where they will be held
- Establish how decisions will be met
- Discuss how this committee will work with others in the library
- Determine how evaluation will be done to improve

EFFECTIVE LISTENING—FIVE BASIC SKILLS TO DEVELOP

Some people are so wrapped up in what they are saying that they may not hear what others are saying. Good supervisors must develop their listening skills and give each person full attention when they are addressing you. There are five basic ways that a person can improve their skills. The first is to listen with your whole body. Your facial expressions and your body movements tell the speaker that you hear him or her, and how well you understand their message. A nod of the head will work for this. The second technique is to give the speaker some verbal signs. Simple phrases such as "I see" or "I understand" convey the message that you are listening. Thirdly, it is important to repeat the message. Again, this technique clarifies what you have heard, and if it is not what the speaker intended they then have the opportunity to restate it. A fourth important step is to listen to the message, not just the words. Perhaps someone is trying to tell you something but they cannot put it into words; this is the same as "reading between the lines." You are actually translating what people say into what they really mean. And last but not least, it is important to summarize or paraphrase the message so that you have the complete intent of the speaker. Utilize these five steps during one-to-one conversations and in group meetings to ensure that you are a good communicator.

SPECIALIZED COMMUNICATIONS: NETWORKING

Most professionals recognize that it is important to keep in touch with other members of the profession. We do this through our professional memberships and attendance at workshops and conferences. It is also important for library staff members to network with others in the community where they work. Every community, be it a city or a college campus, has events, committee meetings or organizations, and other opportunities for people to get to know one another. Sometimes these opportunities are purely social. At other times, the meeting or event has a special issue on which all will be working.

Librarians need to make sure that they participate in these activities. One of the main reasons is that you have the opportunity to meet the "movers and the shakers" in your community, and one never knows when those individuals will be able to assist you at the library with something that comes up. The other reason is that it makes you an ambassador for library services and it gives you the opportunity to explain exactly what the library does. You can demonstrate why the library may be one of the solutions to an issue that has arisen. Now, it is not enough just to attend. You must circulate, talk, and introduce yourself. Don't be shy about doing this. Extending yourself in this way will make you get the most out of your networking experience. Stay in touch with people you meet; greet them at another event. Or, send them some information that you have found at the library that will be helpful to them in what they are doing. They will be really impressed that you remembered your conversation with them, and that you took the time to find something for them. Remain trustworthy; if you say that you are going to do something, then do it. Or have a really good reason why what you promised is not delivered, and explain it. Stay upbeat and positive. Don't criticize the library or individual staff members. If opinions are requested, think before you speak! Be truthful and tactful. For example, if someone comes up to you and says that your library's audio book collection is awful, don't say, "I know. Mary doesn't know what she is doing." Rather, a general statement like, "We can buy only what we can afford" or, "I haven't looked at our collection lately. Please give me some suggestions and I will pass them on" might be much better answers. Being positive and upbeat outside of the library is just as important as it is within the library building inside—maybe even more so.

On the Job Q & A

Q: What is the "why" of good delegation?

A: Delegation may be necessary because you cannot do everything. This process also helps others develop their skills.

ORGANIZING WORK: USING FLOWCHARTS AND PROCESS MAPS

Flowcharts and process maps are useful in identifying and analyzing various processes that are important for the delivery of library service. By representing steps of a task in a pictorial fashion, sometimes it is easier to see inefficiencies within a system. Creating a flowchart can help us and those we supervise visualize the process.

Before starting to map out your process, it is important to identify all of the steps that are involved with a task, who is involved, and whether there is intersection with processes within another department.

Figure 2.7   Checklist: Tips For Creating Effective Flowcharts

■   Have a clear concept of what you want to map out

■   Use broad terms

■   Map it out as it actually works

■   Walk through the process

Then look for the following indicators that will help you evaluate if the process is working properly.

■   Are there bottlenecks where the process slows down? These may indicate that there are unnecessary steps, or some other problem.

■   Are there weak links? Does this mean that staff has not been properly trained or that they are lacking some other necessary resource?

■   Are there steps that add no value to the process, but do add cost? These may be a result of poor planning.

■   Are there too many decisions showing on the diagram? If so, it may be that the process is too complex or convoluted and should be broken down into smaller steps.

■   Are there too many arrows which indicate that the steps have to be reworked back and then sent forward again? Is that really necessary?

Redesigning workflow through this process has many values. It can help your library save time, and also money. Employees feel satisfied when work is done efficiently and they can see progress made, so morale also improves.

DECISION-MAKING

Supervisors are called upon to make decisions all of the time. It would be easier if we had the time to consider all facets of a problem or question. Luckily, sometimes we do. However, there are other times when we are in situations when we have to make a decision very rapidly. If you take the time to learn a simple decision-making process, then you will be equipped to make the decisions when the need arises. It is always important to look closely at the issue at hand when making the decision without losing sight of the big picture. Don't be afraid to use a flowchart or some other diagram if it will help clarify the problem at hand. Following are some suggestions that can help you make decisions in an orderly, logical fashion.

First of all, your task is to define and clarify the problem. Are "symptoms" being shown? Can you get to the cause by breaking the issue down into parts? What is known and what facts do you need to find out before you proceed? What should not be done, considering policy, rules, and past practice? How will the decision impact both short-term and long-term goals?

Secondly, I recommend that you analyze the problem to determine if it is an ethical, moral, professional, or legal one. How long will your decision affect the library? Can your decision be reversed? Is it a recurring problem that is arising that needs a longer-term solution?

Think about all possible solutions. Again, what was done in the past? What are some alternatives? What would be the consequences of using these alternatives? Weigh risks, restrictions, limitations. In other words, think about everything that could go wrong, and have a balanced solution for it. Finally, select the action (decision) that you feel is most appropriate for the situation at hand, and implement it. If it is a decision that you feel needs approval before you proceed, take it through that process as well with your supervisor. Be prepared to tell your supervisor how you reached the decision that you have made and why. Remember, if the problem has been brought to your attention by other staff members, you will want to be very clear in your communication with them of what the library is doing and why, so that they also feel included in the decision-making process.

The key factors that come into play in the decision-making process are the supervisor's authority and experience, whether experimentation (risk-taking) is deemed appropriate, and the amount of analysis that is needed in the process. We should be considering what can be done rather than what cannot. That positive at-

On the Job Q & A

Q: What is the "how" of good delegation?

A: The way in which you delegate may determine if an employee will be successful or not. The following are tips to help you: Give complete instructions; grant sufficient authority; maintain communications; make criticism constructive; reward success.

titude is beneficial in this decision-making process as well. It is important that those who may be affected by the decisions should be involved in the decision-making process if possible, but at the very least informed of the decision at the earliest possible date. As a supervisor, you will be called upon time and again to use "informed judgment." This means that you are expected to make the decisions based on your experience, training, and knowledge.

Some practical suggestions are to distinguish between big problems and little ones. Little ones can usually be solved quickly. You may need to rely on policy and on additional fact-finding for larger issues, and that is also when you may want to have your supervisor look over what you have decided and give his or her approval. It is also a good idea to try to be prepared and have crisis plans in places. This will help you avoid making hasty decisions in the time of crisis and perhaps avoid mistakes. And finally, you cannot expect that you will be "right" all of the time. We all make mistakes. The important thing is to know that we must own up to the mistake, correct the problem, and move on. It serves no purpose to try to defend a bad decision. People will respect you more if you just move on.

Another idea that can be helpful in the decision-making process is to consider who the experts are in a particular area. Is there someone else in your library who may have already made some similar decision? Can you call on a colleague in another library for advice? Or perhaps, from another city department? Have you considered who the people are who are close to the problem? Have you asked them for some of their ideas? Listen with respect to other viewpoints and keep an open mind. Maybe their situation was not the same as yours, but you won't know unless you ask.

Ultimately, you should consider the impact of your decisions on a cumulative basis. These will have an impact on your reputation and your success as a manager.

Remember this: Leaders draw people around themselves and direct them toward their meeting common goals. You cannot lead if people don't follow you!

Figure 2.8   Exercise: Self-Assessment for Management and Leadership Qualities

---

Supervision means leadership as well. The following is a self-analysis exercise that can be helpful to you in understanding your leadership capabilities.

Answer the following questions to help you evaluate what principles are guiding your management style.

1.   What is more important to you—being honest or being the best?

2.   Is it more important to enjoy work or to get the job done no matter what it takes?

3.   What qualifies as a satisfying day at work: everyone working together as a team or meeting a difficult deadline?

4.   Do you think that you should believe that your library's service is the best in order to excel, or do you find personal satisfaction in your own abilities?

5.   Which statement do you agree with most?

    A.   Everyone should get along on the job and work together.
       or
    B.   A little competition among co-workers is a good thing.

The answers to these questions should help you understand a little more about the way that you view management responsibilities. If you selected more of the first choice, then you probably are "people-oriented." Teamwork is a priority for you. If you selected more of the second choice, then you are project-oriented. Under your leadership, people can develop individually if you show them that their abilities will help your organization meet its goals.

THE LIBRARY FACILITY AND THE SUPERVISOR

On the Job Q & A

Q: What steps do I take to solve problems?

A: Problem solving is never easy, but if you do the following you will find your way.

- Define and identify the problem. Get the facts. Develop alternative solutions.
- Pick the *best* solution out of your list. Implement it. Evaluate its effectiveness. If it is not working, go back and try another one of your ideas.

While the management of the facility is usually falls within the Director's responsibility, a supervisor may often have areas of responsibility delegated to him or her, especially if there is no maintenance or janitorial staff on the payroll. This is especially true during evening or weekend shifts. Therefore, it is good practice for supervisors to learn about the basics of the facility's operation so that they are able to keep the library functioning on their watch.

It is a good management practice to have a Supervisor's Notebook that has the necessary forms, emergency and contractor phone lists, policies and procedures available at all times in a readily accessible place.

All supervisors should be familiar with all emergency proceedings including the fire evacuation plan and the workplace injury plan. They should either know first aid assistance, CPR, and AED use, or know whom to call if these services are required. They should know the location of flashlights or lanterns for power failures, a wheelchair and other specialized equipment. All supervisors should know the location of utility controls and how to recognize the warnings or alarms that are associated with these.

Most of all, supervisors need to be able to keep calm and cool and be able to manage the people who are in the library at the time of an unexpected event. This includes staff and public alike. I strongly recommend reading this author's *The Librarian's Facility Management Handbook* for detailed information on all areas of managing a facility. When an unexpected situation arises while you are the supervisor on duty, it is recommended that you file a report with your supervisor as soon as possible. You will, of course, follow local policies and procedures, which may include a phone call to a designated person and/or a written record of the occurrence. Know what is expected of you.

Figure 2.9 shows samples of a written report form that can be used to cover everyday occurrences, and Figure 2.10 shows one for emergency situations.

Figure 2.9   Sample: Supervisor's Report Form

Date:

Supervisor on Duty_____
                          Signature

Facility	**Problem**	**Action Taken:**
Heat		
Air Conditioning		
Lighting		
Plumbing		
Parking Lot		
Meeting Room(s)		
Equipment		
Other _____		

Staff

Absent (list names)

Other _____

Patrons

Complaints

Other

Figure 2.10   Sample: Emergency Incident Report Form

Date:

Supervisor on Duty_____
                            Signature

Incident Information _____

Person _____

Phone _____

Description of Loss/Accident:

_____

_____

_____

Describe Damage:

_____

_____

_____

Patron Information if Involved In Incident: (Name/Phone)

_____

Witness Information: (Name/Phone)

_____

Action Taken: (Police called, Ambulance, etc.)

_____

ABOUT WORKING CONDITIONS

Remember that the physical environment sends a message to employees. While you may feel this is not your role, but the Director's responsibility, a supervisor can do several things that will make people feel that there is concern for them. Many organizations are limited by lack of funds for elegant interior decorating, but we always should remember that employee work areas influence what employees think about where they work and how they are valued. The physical environment communicates how the organization values and is committed to the employee. It should provide a productive, stimulating work environment while meeting the professional needs of the staff. Some strategies include having break rooms that are comfortable and attractive. It is good to display awards and achievements of the library and of individual employees. Likewise, it is attractive and fun to include pictures of historical significance, and displays of future plans and off-site projects. Help all employees find some "space" that is for them alone. You may not be able to provide them with their own desk or office, but a shelf, a message box, a drawer where they can store personal items usually is possible and will make people feel that they are truly a part of the staff.

GIVING DIRECTIONS AND DELEGATION

This sounds simple, right? If you have common sense, and have thought through the work process, then you utilize your communication skills to provide direction. This should be rather simple. However, there are times that we know what we want done, and we know how we would perform a task, but faulty transmission of information can cause a problem. If we are going to include the "ability to follow directions" on our staff evaluations, then we must be sure that we have provided them with a good set of instructions.

First and foremost, it is critical at the outset that you know and tell your employees what the desired results of their tasks are. Set up objectives and process steps. Put the directions in writing and use diagrams if appropriate to help them understand. This is especially useful when introducing a new piece of equipment that requires knowing which wire goes where. Tell them the timing—when you need the tasks completed. Also let them know if

On the Job Q & A

Q: I've just taken a job as the public services manager. One of the employees in the circulation department is consistently late to work. I'm having trouble dealing with her because she has worked here for 15 years and she's older than my mother! Any tips?

A: As the new person, I would have a meeting to go over all of the tasks, policies, etc., that are already in place and ask for input from the staff members regarding these. This technique does not single out any one employee. Yet it lets all know that you are aware of what the policies are and that you expect everyone to abide by them. If the person continues to arrive late, I would ask her privately for the reason why. Does she have to care for an elderly parent before she comes to work? Or is she just taking advantage of the system? During this time, I would also observe her to see what she does well and compliment her on it. You can also try to win her over by acknowledging her 15 years of experience and asking for her assistance.

there is a certain place where you want them to complete tasks. Some tasks may be sensitive, and you may not want people working on them in the public's eye. For example, we all know that we must weed our collections and remove books. Book lovers and the public often have a very hard time with us "destroying items bought with taxpayers' money."

Giving directions is important whenever you delegate work. Many people resist relinquishing control, but delegate you must! Or else you will not be performing the most basic management function of getting work done through others.

Some appropriate tasks to delegate include: information gathering/research, repetitive assignments, developing a training program for others, especially if the staff member has a particular expertise. A detailed task is all examples of good tasks to delegate. It is never a good idea to delegate tasks that involve confidential information, are politically sensitive, or are specifically tied to your performance of management activities.

At times you may begin to believe that your staff is too dependent on you. As their supervisor, you have the right to expect mature behavior from them, and to expect that work that you have delegated be done competently in a timely fashion. This is the time to ask yourself if you have inadvertently encouraged dependency. Have you been unclear in your expectations? Do you discourage people from being independent and from taking responsibility upon themselves? Do you find that staff members "fall apart" when you are not there? While it is flattering to feel so needed, it is unnecessary. You should be preparing your staff to handle routine situations and decisions without you. That is what delegation is. How can you improve on what message you are sending if you identify these problems? First of all, it is not wise to just hand out decisions all the time. If you have a made a decision that affects other people, explain the reason why you have arrived at it. Better yet, ask for their input before you make the decision. Ask them what they think they should do. Try not to show that you may be upset by a decision or you don't agree with it. If it is not harmful, let the staff try it. If the decision that they made then doesn't work, then go back and use this as a learning experience and show people why it doesn't work. Then help the staff to come to a better resolution for the problem at hand. This experience has the added benefit of being staff development for both you and your staff. Chances are, the next time that a similar situation arises, you and they will handle it differently.

Figure 2.11   Steps and Tools to Help You Develop New Skills

At this point, you are probably thinking, "What am I going to do to learn how to do my job?" because supervision really does involve many things that you may not have encountered before. My advice is not to panic; remember that you are a bright, dedicated employee and you will learn how to supervise. Here are some steps you can take to, first, identify your current skill set, and second, find tools that help you acquire new skills.

1.   Ask for feedback from others (your supervisors, peers, people you trust) on your current skills and behaviors.

2.   Decide which skills you think are going to be most important in your new position.

3.   Take stock of yourself. Outline your strengths and weaknesses as honestly as you can.

4.   Identify those key development target areas—areas where you would like to improve.

5.   Investigate various methods of helping yourself improve. These may involve taking a workshop or seminar; taking an additional college course; shadowing a "seasoned" supervisor; reading books on supervision techniques, etc.

6.   Determine a method of monitoring your own progress on your development. Include asking for feedback again as one of the ways.

What are some of the tools that can be useful in helping you develop new skills? Sometimes they are things that we do every day, but we have not placed the value on them that we should have. Here are some suggestions.

1. READ!!! While it is important that you keep current with the professional literature of our field, it is also very valuable to read a variety of materials. Books, annual reports, and journals from the corporate business world offer many good suggestions that can be adapted to library management. Because they are coming from a different perspective, they have the tendency to encourage you to look at things from a different perspective and to "think out of the box."

2. Self-monitor! Use written goals and objectives. These may be what you have determined along with your supervisor, or they may be your own personal goals. The process of writing them down is the process of making a "contract"

of sorts with yourself. Then, establish a tracking system that will be able to rate the amount of progress that you are making toward your objectives. Keep a log, and use a simple indicator such as a checkmark (√) so that you can see your progress at a glance.

3. Do not be shy about asking your supervisor to monitor your progress. You will want and need ongoing guidance, especially in areas that you have identified as needing improvement.

4. Take advantage of all training opportunities. Take a formal course. This is especially appropriate if you need to learn some new, complex skills. Classroom learning works best when it is tied to your real needs on the job. Also look for workshops and seminars in areas that you want to improve. Professional associations and your state library often offer free programs or programs at little cost.

5. In libraries as in many other fields, research has proven that the most effective tool for training and development is the job setting itself. This will work for you if you set milestones for yourself. If you write out a development plan, keep it handy. Consult it frequently, and observe areas that you are not improving. Then find ways to develop these skills as well.

DEALING WITH STRESS

At the same time that you are learning how to be a supervisor, you are aware that you are being evaluated by your supervisors. They are looking at what you may be doing to implement change, what work is getting done, how you are adhering to a policy, how you are planning, how you are treating people, and how you are getting along with others.

No one said that the job was going to be easy. This new role does put a strain on you. The new position causes demands. You may feel isolated, especially if you have been promoted from within and your peers now look at you in a new light. The usual reaction is to feel tension and stress.

Stress means different things to different people. There are a number of very good books that can be useful in this situation, so I will not go into detail here. I am also not a counselor, so I do not feel that I am qualified to provide you with specific psychological advice. However, I do think it is appropriate to say that each of us has to find those methods that help us cope with stressful situations, and make sure that we utilize them. That being said, Chapter 9 will provide you with a few sample exercises that can help you cope.

Figure 2.12 Checklist: Becoming the Supervisor You Want To Be

Think back to your first job, then to any other job that you have held since. Answer these questions. At the end of the exercise, you should be able to remember some of the characteristics that you now want to portray to the people you supervise and perhaps some things you don't!

1.   Did your supervisor make you feel glad to be there?

2.   What kind of training did you receive?

3.   What kind of training do you wish you had received?

4.   What kind of mistakes did you make? How did your supervisor respond to them?

5.   What would have been most helpful to you during the first days on the job?

6.   What was your biggest fear when you started your job?

7.   Who helped you overcome that fear? How? What did they do?

8.   Based on your experience, what is the number one thing that you want to do for new employees when they come to work for you?

At this point in your reading, you may again be feeling a little overwhelmed because you are now finding out many of the myriad things you may be called upon to do as part of the administrative hierarchy. But, you are taking action. Doing is what leads to becoming, and as you progress through this book, you will become more and more comfortable with the role that you are now playing as a supervisor. In fact, you will have become one.

3 CREATING AND RUNNING WORK TEAMS

For many years, management was based on what is known as a hierarchical structure. This is a "top-down," pyramid model, in which the people in charge—i.e., the supervisors or bosses—made the decisions. They then handed them down to the workers, who did as they were told. At the top of this pyramid was upper management, followed by middle management, and then lower management. Front-line workers were always on the bottom. Directions and orders filtered down from the top, through each layer, until they reached the workers at the bottom. This type of model suggested that the people at the top knew everything, and the people at the bottom, very little. Also, this structure was purposely designed so that people reported only to the individual directly above them. This often created a very narrow information flow and discouraged cooperation and communication among people in the workplace. In fact, miscommunication was very common.

Modern business environments recognize that the workplace is much more efficient and productive when more people have information and when ideas are shared. In libraries especially, our work is often cross-functional, and the best solutions are found when everyone works together.

Today, teamwork is the foundation, and is in fact the preferred practice of successful library management, as well as other contemporary businesses. Our workplaces are becoming more and more complicated with information overflow, and with a society that demands immediate satisfaction. We now recognize that the employees closest to the actual delivery of service have the expertise, knowledge, and perspective that can make a difference in the success of an organization. This is especially true when various talents are pooled. Therefore, front-line staff should be encouraged to make decisions.

Because information continues to expand, and technologies continue to change, all staff members will continue to require ongoing training. The use of teamwork to manage the competitive pressures placed on us by these forces can be a highly effective method of dealing with them. Training helps improves technical skills, but it also helps with the development of managerial and interpersonal skills. This is especially true when one or more staff members use teamwork to do in-house training. The skills developed often eliminate weaknesses within the organization. But, they also serve to reinforce existing and still necessary skills, while they foster the development of new ones for future opportunities. Teamwork in itself provides an opportunity for personal growth and learning. Teams can create a sense of energy and enthusiasm in the workplace. Teamwork is more than a fad or buzzword. Most people find that their whole work attitude changes when they are able to contribute their ideas and opinions. Individuals feel a sense of accomplishment when they see that their team's solutions are working effectively. They develop self-esteem, and value themselves. Thus teamwork becomes a true business advantage.

Employees who are on the "front line" of library service have developed the expertise, knowledge, and the necessity of multiskilled practices. However, bringing individual employees together as a work team can still be a challenge for the supervisor as well as for the employee. While the benefits of teamwork are many, it can be frustrating if discussions during team meetings are off the subject, or if meetings drag on, or if an agenda is not followed. The supervisor has the responsibility of intervening so this does not happen. This is not only because valuable time can be wasted, but also because the team members may become bored. Yet, the dynamic forces that are the results of good teamwork are important in solving problems, in improving processes, and in developing new services. So, it is worth the effort that the supervisor puts in to oversee the work of the team.

When teams meet, members discuss their objective, and they make decisions and work toward their goals together. By definition, the team is a group of people working together to reach a goal that everyone believes in. Team members must be highly committed to the process and mutually accountable. Everyone understands that it would be difficult, if not impossible, to achieve the goal by working alone.

Teams must be small enough to allow free discussion among all of their members. All successful teams possess the following features: strong and effective leadership, precise objectives, the know-how to make informed decisions, and open communications. The supervisor will want to make sure that the members will be able to bring a balance of emphasis between the technical content and the team process to the table. It is in this way that team members reinforce one another so that the seemingly impossible becomes doable.

Creating work teams to accomplish particular tasks is an important part of a supervisor's job. Once established, the supervisor has the task of nurturing the team and keeping it focused on the work at hand. As a new supervisor, it is important that you develop the interpersonal skills that are needed to be a team leader, if necessary. You must learn when it is appropriate for you to become involved and know when to keep away. In order to help teams achieve success, the supervisor must to be able to recognize and to balance the people skills within a team that will be working independently, making suggestions that are helpful while not taking over. A valued manager is one who is flexible and is able to shift from one thing to another.

Sometimes teams will need your help "now," no matter what else you are doing. You will also have to make decisions about when it would be productive to use a team to accomplish a task, and when situations demand that work be performed independently. The following is a list of when it would be useful to establish a work team.

WHY YOU WOULD USE TEAMWORK IN THE WORKPLACE

- Top management cannot make every decision
- Work is getting more and more complex
- Someone has up-to-date knowledge that needs to be shared
- Increase productivity; more is accomplished
- Resources (people, dollars, and time) are used more efficiently
- Improve quality of work
- Improve communication
- Involve many in decision-making process; people feel better about work when they have a say in the way things are done
- People will need to take responsibility for implementing changes
- Increases creativity in the workplace
- Examine systems and practices to improve services
- Group synergy will be the most effective way to complete the task

The following are some important skills that people should have in order to be effective team players. If you have employees who do not have these skills, then it becomes your responsibility to help them acquire them, or to hire other staff members who have them already.

QUALITIES FOR GOOD TEAM MEMBERS

- Ability to speak up
- Ability to listen
- Be willing to take risks—you want new ideas and the courage to try them out
- Strongly motivated
- Helpful
- Reliable
- Consistently meet commitments
- Have common sense
- Have some technical expertise
- Respect others viewpoints
- Willing to try to make things a success
- Efficient
- Energetic
- Inspire trust in themselves and trust others
- Willing to support others on the team
- Cope well with interpersonal skills
- Ability to make decisions

The supervisor has a purpose when he or she decides that a work team should be established. However, for the team to really develop, the members themselves must ask the following questions.

QUESTIONS EVERY TEAM WILL ASK OF ITSELF

- What is our purpose?   (mission)
- What do we stand for?   (the philosophy/value system)
- Who are we?   (our culture)
- Where do we want to go?   (objectives/goals)

As a way to provide some guidance without taking over, supervisors may find it useful to have their employees complete the following self-assessment exercise before assigning them to a work team. This gives employees the opportunity to honestly question their own behavior before they enter the process. As the team building process begins, the members will be better able to understand and adjust their own behavior as situations develop.

On the Job Q & A

Q: Help! The work team I created seems to have all leaders and no team players! What do I do?

A: Look for a film by Ken Blanchard called "Workteams and the Wizard of Oz" (CRM Films, 1997). This film shows how things can be accomplished more efficiently with teams. It brings an element of fun to the workplace, and is literature-based! Most people admit that they never viewed this film in this light before, and the various roles that are necessary to make a team function are very clearly illustrated. This film helps people recognize what is not working in their own situation.

Figure 3.1   Checklist: Self-Assessment for Teamwork Concepts

1. How important do you believe it is to arrive at team meetings on time?

    _____Extremely   _____Somewhat   _____Not Very Important

2. How important do you believe it is to be prepared for the team's work focus?

    _____Extremely   _____Somewhat   _____Not Very Important

3. How important is it to ask for and to welcome suggestions from other team members rather than trying to solve a problem by yourself?

    _____Extremely   _____Somewhat   _____Not Very Important

4. In an instance of conflict among team members, how important is it to identify the root source of the issue as opposed to fixing the problem with a temporary solution?

    _____Extremely   _____Somewhat   _____Not Very Important

5. How important is it to share ideas and feedback with other team members and doing it openly, honestly, and compassionately, putting personal feelings aside?

    _____Extremely   _____Somewhat   _____Not Very Important

6. How important is it to acknowledge the contributions of other team members and to make sure that they are recognized for their efforts?

    _____Extremely   _____Somewhat   _____Not Very Important

7. How important is it to treat all members of the team with respect and dignity even though you may not agree with their ideas or their approach to the problem?

    _____Extremely   _____Somewhat   _____Not Very Important

8. How important is it to put the interest of the group first, as opposed to your own self-interest?

    _____Extremely   _____Somewhat   _____Not Very Important

There have been many studies that evaluate the various roles that individuals take on during team meetings. Some of these are related to particular tasks that must be done; others are related to the process. Depending on the size of the group and the actual situations, people may actually take on more than one of the roles simultaneously. Some of the roles that are specific to tasks include the "opinion givers." These are people who freely offer their opinion to the group. There are others who seeks out information and often ask for clarification. If a team leader or chair has not been selected, someone will inevitably assume that role. In actuality, there are three scenarios regarding leaders for work teams. First of all, there is the implied leader. This may be you as the supervisor, or another individual who has the rank, or expertise, to take on the role. Or, there may be an emergent leader. This is someone who earns the role during the team deliberations, especially if the supervisor steps back. The third type of leader is the "designated leader." This is someone who is either appointed or elected when the group is formed. This will be the person who coordinates the team meetings and provides some direction for the group work. The leader may suggest an agenda or strategies to proceed with the task on hand. While we are lucky that some people are willing to talk in groups, there are some other people who are reluctant to share their opinions. The leader's task is to see that they not only have the opportunity to contribute, but also to call upon them and encourage their contribution. Other roles that are found in groups include someone who takes on the task of analyzing what is happening; the analyzer might suggest solutions to a problem, or ways to implement them. At other times, an important role may be to question the direction in which a group is moving. Teams, especially ones that tackle ongoing issues, need members to energize them; their role is ongoing encouragement and keeping the goal in sight. We should not underestimate this very important role. Sometimes the leader, but in other cases a team member, takes on the role of summarizer. This process makes the team members take stock of what they are doing and where they are in the process of achieving their goal. This role may be extended to that of an evaluator as well, because the group will need to measure their accomplishments against standards that are particular to the task at hand.

In regard to process, one role that must be assumed is that of communicator. This role ensures that all positions are heard and understood. Active listening is as important as speaking, and feedback is provided to the other members of the team so that they know their voices are being heard. Strong communications are important to inform, to persuade others to one's point of view, to encourage others to speak up, and to get people to change their minds. Communications are most effective when they are personal, informal, and direct. It is inevitable that personalities will clash and differences of opinion will cause tension. Team members, with the leader, must work to understand one another's points of view, and encourage everyone to get along on the team. Members may not become best friends outside of the team, but working to overcome differences to reach a goal is a growth experience. And finally, every group needs someone who is able to help reconcile the various points of view, suggesting ways to relieve tension so that group cohesiveness is improved. Supervisors can help teams get off to a good start by orchestrating the right mix of staff experience. They may need to intervene during the process if tension or stress is inhibiting progress. This is vital for team effectiveness.

TEAM ATTRIBUTES

Following are some of the attributes that individuals must have in order to take on some of the above-mentioned roles.

Team Leader or Coordinator is the person who needs to be a facilitator and an inspirer. After solutions are agreed on, he or she needs to be able to implement them. However, the team leader does not "control" the group. Team leaders have vision. They are good listeners as well as good speakers. They are confident, loyal, and courageous. They possess a high degree of integrity and are attentive and focus on details. Team leaders are good at inspiring others and at sustaining enthusiasm among people. The team leader is usually the person who is good at heading off trouble as well. This is a person who encourages the group to set priorities and is able to show how various tasks interrelate. A team leader stimulates problem-solving. The facilitator helps the team learn about itself; observes and watches for nonverbal cues; and probes and provides feedback, especially when other members are hesitant to speak.

Idea People are always enthusiastic and lively. These are positive, hopeful people who sees problems as opportunities. They keep searching for different ways of doing things, and while every idea might not be a valid one, their enthusiasm is catching to other participants. *Critics* are analytical types. Critics are usually never satisfied with less than the best. They will point out every way that something could go wrong. They can be merciless, but their analysis often leads to constructive solutions. *Inspectors* are people who have good judgment; very often they make the group adhere to standards and rules. *Implementers* possess good time management skills. They keep everyone on a schedule, and have a methodical "can-do" attitude.

There are three types of needs that must be fulfilled in all groups in order for them to be successful. Someone must assume each of these responsibilities and they don't always fall under the above-mentioned roles. The first set of needs is known as *procedural*. These are logistical details which include when and where to meet; who will set an agenda, prepare handouts, start the meeting, summarize what happens during the meeting and end the meeting. *Tasks* needs are the distribution of the workload that is necessary for the team to be successful. These include information collection; substantive action needed to help the team complete its work; keeping the focus; playing devil's advocate; formulating criteria to judge for the most effective solutions; helping the team reach final consensus and recommendations for action. Finally, there are the ongoing *maintenance* needs that ensure that communications are happening and that the interpersonal relationships between the group members are on a stable level. The distribution of these responsibilities will vary by team and workplace. They will also vary based on the intensity of the supervisor's participation in the process. In either case, these are areas that must be considered if work teams are going to be successful.

Interpersonal relations are another important area that must be considered during the team-building process. Team members need to learn how to adjust their behavior to one another. Everyone must understand that there are effects that result from various personality styles and from the different ways that people approach situations. All team members must remember that how they think they appear to others may indeed be different from the way that they are viewed. Do we speak up, or are we considered loud? Are we quiet and reserved, or are we not participating? Are we friendly and smiling, or are we aloof or shy, not giving anyone eye contact? Before we can interact successfully with others, we truly need to take stock of our own behavior and be aware and sensitive to others. While team members are not expected to change their personality, accommodations and considerations must be made for people to get along with one another.

Versatility is a key in adapting to others. Because discussion is one of the most significant components of teamwork, let us look at the following example as a versatile way of approaching potential interpersonal conflict.

Many of us are already familiar with one tool that is often used

On the Job Q & A

Q: I find that team members do not communicate well with one another. Any suggestions?

A: Take a hint from Salvador Dali! Divide the team into groups of two. Give them each something to write with and something to write on. Give one person a picture of five different boxes. The goal is for that person to direct the other person to draw the boxes without seeing the picture. This is not an easy exercise. However, It does make people reexamine their communication skills.

in teamwork sessions, which can test our versatility and flexibility. "Brainstorming" is when members of a group randomly call out ideas. Usually these ideas are listed on a blackboard or flip chart. And after all have had their say, the team goes back over them, grouping ideas together if appropriate, then prioritizing them for discussion/action. Try to recall when you have been in one of these sessions before. It is hard not to disagree sometimes, isn't it? However, if you let the process work through, all members get their say. If open discussions are held, the best results and ideas usually surface. And sometimes one idea generates another idea. If someone interrupts or disagrees with an idea in the beginning stages of brainstorming, it often has the effect of stifling discussion, or maybe even developing conflict between team members. Also, if you are in a situation where it seems that some members are not participating, you might want to suggest an alternate method for starting discussion. In this method, every member takes blank paper and anonymously writes down his or her ideas. Those papers are then given to one person who reads them out loud, and the discussion list is shared with all. This works very well if there are some shy or hesitant people in a group who might not otherwise contribute. It is also a way to keep that "overachiever" participant from controlling the discussion. Most often I have found that these overachievers do not realize that they are monopolizing the situation.

The checklist in Figure 3.2 is one that team members can use to assess whether their behavior is constructive. Again, many of us don't even realize how our behavior may be impacting the group. Depending on the results of this checklist, some team members may have to change their role in the team structure in order to bring their points across to others.

Figure 3.2   Checklist: Promoting Team Building Behavior

■ Confronting—Team members insist that the team deals with issues that it appears it may want to avoid

■ Gatekeeping—All members have the opportunity to contribute

■ Mediating—Some members have taken on the role of intervening in disputes among two or more members

■ Harmonizing—members look for areas of agreement among two or more members of the group

■ Supporting—Reinforce the right of any group member to speak or to have his or her opinion heard

■ Summarizing—Someone takes the time to bring together the various contributions so that there is a checkpoint for balance.

Likewise, there are behaviors that may cause groups not to focus on the issue at hand. These are not helpful to helping the team reach its goal, and again, we each should identify if there are areas in which we need to change.

Figure 3.3   Checklist: Identifying Obstructive Team Behaviors

- Shutting off: This is when one member silences another by interrupting, changing the subject, or by putting down another's idea.

- Analyzing: Team members should not "label" or suggest motives for another team member's behavior.

- Dominating: Team work is group work. If one member dominates the meeting with his or her ideas or opinions, it means that this person has also prevented other members from contributing.

- "Yes-But": With this behavior, someone seems to agree with an idea or an opinion, but then proceeds to argue against it.

- Nay-saying: This is negative behavior, where a team member discounts an idea or opinion before it is given a chance to be considered. The classic, "We tried that and it didn't work," is an example of this type of behavior.

One of the temptations that a supervisor may have when forming work teams is to pass over people who tend to "play devil's advocate." This might seem comforting—it would avoid any confrontation in the work session. However, people who "make waves" often put out ideas that should be addressed. For the long-term good of the team and its development of solutions, it is a good idea to have all different viewpoints represented. It is important that team members are able to confront these tough issues. Conflict provides the team members with the opportunity to understand other points of view. So, polite confrontation actually aids the teamwork process. However, what the supervisor will have to watch for are behaviors that are so extreme that they might block the group process. These may include premature decision-making, which happens when some members of the group make decisions or reach a conclusion before all the facts are in. Another blocking behavior is when someone presents opinions as facts. It is absolutely essential that facts are documented and opinions are clearly identified as such.

Sometimes group members wander off the focused discussion. They may talk about things that are unrelated to the topic, or cite their own personal experiences that may not be relevant. Some people analyze things too much, or argue just to argue. There are some who will purposely take the opposite position from other members of the group. Some go so far as being aggressive and attacking others and their ideas. Others may be judgmental; they view situations only on the basis of their own beliefs; they may also reject ideas because of their attitude toward the person who is presenting them. The supervisor then may have the responsibility of intervening so that these blocking behaviors will not hinder the team process. As the supervisor, you may have to help the team enforce its own rules and procedures so that decisions are made on facts by individuals who have remained flexible and open-minded.

CHARACTERISTICS OF A GOOD TEAM

Collectively, individuals must come together in order to address the work of the team. The following are the characteristics that teams need in order to be successful.

- There is a shared purpose or a common goal that is understood by all team members. Teams bring together people with different talents, abilities, experiences, and backgrounds.
- People must work together and encourage one another to contribute. If someone has made the decision that a team is the way to achieve a particular goal, then all team members must understand that people will need other people in order to achieve it. People will expect to be exposed to different points of view and recognize that their combined brainpower will be pooled to overcome obstacles.
- Directly, or indirectly, there must be some perceivable benefit to all, even if people are assigned to the team. This is what will make them committed to the process. Perhaps it is job satisfaction, it is good for their self-esteem, or they learn something new, or they just have fun!
- Teams just don't meet; they act on the recommendations that they develop.
- Teams must recognize the value of consensus. In order for this to happen, all members must feel that their point

of view has been heard and understood. They must be able to "live" with the decision that has been made, and they must also be willing to pull together so that the decision actually becomes reality.

- Good teams avoid misunderstanding by documenting meetings through minutes, outlines, or recorded comments. Written minutes assure clarity of each member's contributions as well as the decisions that are made.

If supervisors have the opportunity to utilize teamwork, they have an opportunity to guide and develop people, a task that is much more rewarding than giving orders. The supervisor's main role is to model the behavior and the attitudes that they want to see team members exhibit. Following is a list of positive behaviors that a supervisor should show.

SUPERVISOR'S ROLE IN TEAMWORK

- Determines if teamwork makes sense for the task at hand
- Vocalizes common goal and its organizational impact
- Develops team player skills among employees
- Creates an environment that is conducive to teamwork
- Fosters innovation and initiative
- Provides resources necessary for the team's success
- Makes sure that all know their responsibilities
- Evaluates strengths and weaknesses of the team
- May contribute ideas and expertise when appropriate
- Makes sure that all contribute to the discussion
- May help the group reach consensus
- Ensures commitment in implementing decisions
- Ask members if they are satisfied with the process
- Listens
- Is reliable and carries through on promises
- Is congenial, courteous, and considerate
- Is supportive and encouraging
- Praises when appropriate
- Resolves conflict among team members
- Anticipates barriers that may impede team's effectiveness and looks for ways to overcome them
- Is consistent and predictable
- Is a cheerleader and counsels and coaches the team
- Inspires and motivates employees

- Rewards critical thinking
- Credits participants, shows appreciation, and publicizes the team's success

If the supervisor is going to delegate to a work team, and not be its leader, then he or she must be certain to delegate fully. This means giving the team members full responsibility for the task at hand. It means empowering them so that they can optimize member' contributions and then execute the solutions that they have developed. The supervisor must prepare the team and give them a very clear focus on what the library's vision and direction is before assigning them a task. The team will then move on to develop the goals and objectives that meet this vision. The supervisor continues to monitor their progress, and intervenes only when the actions that the team has taken have not allowed them to reach their objective because, ultimately, they are accountable for the results.

In summary, the supervisor lets the team know about the directions and the priorities. He or she lets the team decide what to do and how to do it. The supervisor checks on the team's progress and provides advice or suggestions for corrective action if the team is faltering. When the team has accomplished its task, the supervisor should provide recognition and rewards that acknowledge these team achievements. "Winning" teams just don't happen. As the "coach," you, the supervisor, will show them the way!

BASIC INFORMATION POINTS ABOUT TEAMWORK

- Goals are shared; they must be measurable goals, so that progress can be seen
- People must work together
- Teamwork should benefit all involved
- Teams work best when there is an effective mix of skills and strengths
- Teamwork is a way of making priorities clear
- Team members agree on "rules" that govern their activity
- Team members must be willing to participate and cooperate
- Teams build trust among members; this translates into

       credibility, reliability, fairness, and truthfulness of team members

- Members are committed to consensus
- Team members are still individuals and need to be treated as such
- Laughter brings people together and is a great stress reducer
- Key to an effective team meeting is to actively involve everyone in the proceedings
- Team members trust that their supervisor supports their actions

TYPES OF WORK TEAMS

Before a team is selected for a task, there are some important points that must be considered. First of all, the type of team that is put in place is clearly dictated by the task at hand. In some cases, *cross-functional* teams are appropriate. In a library setting, this might be a team of supervisors who represent all departments and branches. They will meet on a regular schedule, and discuss day-to-day operational issues. This type of team pools together various levels and specialties of expertise. The combined knowledge of the group is used to develop solutions for problems. The cross-functional team is also very good for the library because it gives people the chance to learn about the various roles and work that others are doing in the library. For example, the children's librarian learns about the ordering and cataloging process. Then, there is an understanding that the books that were ordered from their department might take two months to appear. On the same level, if the children's library needs them for a summer reading program, the acquisitions department might then understand that they need to be given priority status. The teamwork in this area breaks down barriers; staff members realize that they have the same goal—to get the books out to the patrons. This type of cross-functional team is one that is ongoing.

Process-improvement teams are similar to cross-functional teams in the problem-solving area. However, these are usually formed within one department in order to focus on a problem that is specific to that department or function. It is still a good idea to select members with varying amounts of experiences as well as different skills for this type of team. This ensures balance and different viewpoints.

A *project* team is one that is called together for a specific task, such as a building construction project. Subgroups may also form under this type of team to carry out a particular function. This group dissolves when the project is completed. Again, having a varied representation of experience, job function, and in the case of building projects, trustees and community members, is very important.

A *change* team is one that has the specific purpose of changing the way things are currently being done. Members of this type of group need to be carefully selected by the specific skills that they bring to the table. Because the solutions that they suggest will influence the way things will be done in the future, they will need to have the common goal of bringing others to their point of view.

A *management* team oversees other teams. It provides the oversight, the direction of vision, the resources, and the removal of barriers that might prevent project teams or cross-functional teams from meeting their objectives. Usually, these individuals are on the team based on their job function or title.

Quality circles are specific problem-solving and process-improvement teams that operate on a continual basis. Instead of making drastic changes occasionally, quality circles function continually to develop sometimes small but important incremental changes to improve processes and services.

In any case, the process of full participation and open discussion is vital for the success of any of these models. We refer you to the author's earlier book, *Successful Staff Development* (New York: Neal-Schuman, 1995, pp. 68–69) for a Teamwork Training Curriculum.

Figure 3.4   Sample: Open-Ended Team Discussion Questions

These are some sample questions that can be used to encourage discussion among team members. They are general in nature; however, you can use them as a guideline to prepare questions that would be useful to the particular assignment that you are giving a team.

A.   Questions to FOCUS Discussion

1.   Where are we right now in relation to our goal?

2.   Would someone give their interpretation of what we have said so far so we can all be on the same page?

3.   That comment is interesting, but can you help me understand how it is relevant to our task?

B.   Questions to MOVE the Team Ahead

1.   Does everyone feel that we have spent enough time talking about this aspect of the issue? Should we move onto something else now?

2.   Should we give some time to _____ (specific) area?

3.   Since we have a time limit, would it be wise to look at other aspects of the issues? We can come back to this later if we feel the need.

C.   Team Self-Evaluation Questions

1.   Should we go back and revisit our charge to see if we are on the right track?

2.   We seem blocked on this issue. What might move us along?

3.   Since we are near the end of our meeting, is there anything we haven't covered today? Should it be done now or the next time we meet?

4.   Does anyone have any suggestions on how to improve our next session?

D.   Questions that Foster Decision-Making

1.   Would someone summarize what we've done already?

2.   What else needs discussion before we make a decision?

3.   What other information or resources do we need for our next session?

4.   Is there anything we need to do on our own before we meet again?

MODEL PROCESS FOR TEAM DECISION-MAKING

Although it is not always easy, teams must arrive at decisions in order to complete their tasks. Compromise is one way of reaching a decision that people can live with. However, the word itself implies that something is given up and then the decision doesn't always meet everyone's expectations. Therefore, it is not the best way for a team to make a decision. Consensus, on the other hand, is a way of getting people with different points of view to see something in a similar way. The requirement of a consensus decision is that the point of view of each member is considered, discussed, compared, and sometimes, even discussed again. Then all team members believe that it is truly the best way to go considering the circumstances.

The following model is the progression of steps that a team should follow in order to achieve the goal.

1. Introductions
   In small libraries, this might not be necessary, but in larger systems it often is. However, a creative supervisor might want to offer an activity or an icebreaker to bring people together as the team, and this would be the appropriate time to do it.
   It is also wise to establish the ground rules before plunging into the problem. All team members must agree to comply with these. This small introductory step may make a huge difference in avoiding conflict later on.
2. Identify the task at hand
   It is absolutely critical that everyone be very clear on the purpose of the team and what is expected of it during the process.
3. Information gathering
   This should be easy for us in our profession! What are the facts and other information and/or resources that are needed by the team before a decision can be reached? (For example, Purpose of team discussion: Can we provide Sunday hours at the library? Information needed: Will we be able to hire additional employees? Will all employees be required to work the hours? Will this be negotiated with a union? What other costs are involved—utilities, security, etc.)

On the Job Q & A

Q: The concept of teamwork is fairly new in my library, and the employees are resisting it. What can I do?

A: A good way to illustrate the benefit of teamwork is to use the "quiz bowl" format. Don't forget, librarians love to show off their knowledge. Compile a list of library trivia questions—especially things that are particular to your library. First, ask the employees to answer the questions themselves, without consulting teammates or any other resources. Give them five minutes or so, then ask them to stop. Then group them into small teams and let them answer the rest of the questions. It is amazing how many more questions people will now get answered with cooperative consultation. This little exercise demonstrates the value of teamwork, and you can then emphasize how much more the library will accomplish with strong teams.

4. Brainstorm (or brain-write) various alternate ways to achieve the goal. (For example, flexible schedules; closing some hours during the week; have Sunday only staff.)
5. Ask questions
   Have we considered all possible alternatives?
   Have we looked at this from all perspectives?
6. Solution finding
   The team members would look at all of the pros and the cons of each of the alternative ideas. They would then come to a consensus on which ideas would be best and why.
7. Implementation: This is putting the plan into action.
8. Evaluation
   The team needs to check itself to see if the process of reaching the decision was correct or flawed. They will also need to check to see if the solution is working, or if they need to implement another of the solutions.

Teams must collaborate to be successful. Practice is one of the best ways that we have to improve any skill. Figure 3.6 has some examples of how to improve collaboration skills.

Figure 3.5   Checklist: Tips for Improving Collaboration Skills

If you want to . . .	Then . . .
Listen with interest and respect	Use body language, lean in, nod head
If you want to . . . Actively listen	**Then . . .** Allow others to complete statements without interruption.
If you want to . . . Support interesting ideas	**Then . . .** Find best characteristic even if unorthodox. Support, expand, and encourage to keep on explaining.
If you want to . . . Record all ideas	**Then . . .** Use flip chart or blackboard. Ask to go beyond obvious. Stretch imagination, be creative.
If you want to . . . Collect a great number of ideas	**Then . . .** Collect as many ideas as possible; prioritize later
If you want to . . . Allow time for thinking	**Then . . .** Take break, shake up routine, move furniture
If you want to . . . Ask critics for suggestions	**Then . . .** Encourage participation to "buy in" Do action research Act like a patron. Visit where action will happen
If you want to . . . Ask "what if" questions	**Then . . .** Remove constraints, change perceptions, dream
If you want to . . . Avoid judgment of ideas	**Then . . .** Remember guidelines Treat all respectfully
If you want to . . . Have fun	**Then . . .** Bring food, use humor, and celebrate productive team meetings

---

Figure 3.6   Exercise: Work Team Self-Evaluation of Team Approach

Each employee on the team should be asked to complete this exercise so that they gain a better understanding of how they act within a work group. It is intended for their personal use. They will be much more forthcoming with their answers if they know at the outset that they will not have to share this exercise with anyone else.

Directions: From past team/group experience, please answer the following questions. When you are done, think about your answers and how they might impact a group's performance.

1. How would you identify your behavioral style? Are you aggressive and driving? Friendly and amicable? Analytical and critical? Enthusiastic and supportive? Other?

2. Can you identify a situation in which you carried your style a little too far? Do you know why you did this?

3. Did this overuse of your style cause any problems with the work of the team? Did it diminish the team's effectiveness?

4. Did you observe other team members overdoing their style or role? How did their behavior affect the team? What impact did their behavior have on your behavior? Why?

5. Did this team member cause the team to be less effective? How or why?

There are some potential problems that may arise that will hamper the team from success if they are not addressed. It may be that a key person has not been put on the team. Or it may be that there are individual behaviors that are causing difficulties; team members might arrive late, or leave early, or have not come to the meeting prepared. Long, drawn-out discussions are usually not productive, nor is unfounded complaining, or people who see if they can talk the most or the loudest. Figure 3.8 is an objective exercise that helps identify some of these potential problems.

Remember, the effectiveness of the team is directly related to all the team members taking *responsibility* for the work of the team. The discussion that follows this exercise should be based on that premise. If you are the supervisor involved with the team, this may be the right time for you to intervene to assist the team in making progress. They will want help from you in order to make the team work. However, in the long run it would be better if you could guide them to finding their own solutions, rather than telling them how to fix their problems.

Figure 3.7 Exercise: Work Team SWOT Analysis

A critical function of management is the ability to recognize the Strengths, Weaknesses, Opportunities, and Threats in their organization. In business management, this is the classic "SWOT" analysis. As in business, SWOT is a very valuable tool that teams can use to strengthen themselves.

Directions: All team members should individually complete the following questions. Then they should discuss the results together. Their answers are confidential to their team, and should be given in the spirit of cooperation and team building.

The answers should not be personal attacks on any other team member.

1. What are our team's strengths?

2. What are our team's weaknesses?

3. Are there behavioral or personality imbalances that are impeding our team's performance?

4. Is our team making a contribution to the library?

5. What are some of the obstacles (threats) that are impeding us from reaching our goal?

6. Is there any resource (person, materials, technology, etc.) that we need (i.e., opportunity) that would make a difference in our team fulfilling its purpose?

7. Are we utilizing the individual strengths of each team member as we work on attaining our goal?

8. Are members on time for the meetings?

9. Are members prepared for the meetings? Is everyone contributing equally?

10. Are the meetings organized? If not, what can we do?

11. What happens when team members disagree? Is there more cooperation or more conflict?

12. Are people committed to the decisions, even after the meeting? Do they feel good about the team?

Regardless of how much we prepare, there inevitably will be some problems with work teams. The following is a chart that identifies some of the problems that might occur, and how to identify them when they do. If you address the cause, you might be able to develop a solution that is acceptable to all and will keep the team functioning.

Figure 3.8   Checklist: Strategies to Improve Teams

Here are some practical examples of how to improve the function of work teams.

Use "tools"
- agenda
- constitution/rules (policies or procedures on how to conduct business)
- stop watch/clock for time
- adequate meeting space

Test or pilot solutions
- "tentative" decisions
- identify specific action plan to make changes

Have "supportive" environment
- dedicate adequate time to the process
- openness is promoted
- provide resources

Team rewards
- thank you for participating
- party to celebrate a significant achievement

Figure 3.9	Checklist: Dealing with Team Problems		
Problem	**What You See**	**Possible Causes**	**Potential Solutions**
Lack of disagreement	Ideas accepted with with little discussion	No interest Lack of honesty	Agree to Disagree
Commitment tapers off	Skip meetings No support for ideas	Ground rules not clear Doesn't see benefits	Open rule discussion Supervisor intervention
Open conflict	Emotions on display	Blaming, negative Comments	Conflict resolution
Ideas flat Unoriginal	No thinking time Minimal effort	No creativity No brainstorming	Collaboration Skills and Innovation rewarded
Rumbling	Lots of talk No new ideas	Loss of focus	Summarization Consensus
Individuals	Impasse	Facts or opinions	Consensus
Are inflexible	Emotions		Cooperation
No implementtion	Criticism no changes	Need clear decisions	Confrontation Compliance based on consensus
Unrealistic expectations	Too much change too quickly	Directions not clear	Collaboration
Stakeholders uninformed	Missing information	Lack of communication	Collaboration

In conclusion, work teams have an important role to play in today's libraries. In addition to all of the uses we have already discussed, teams are also important for satisfying the need for socialization among people. Working together helps people grow as they learn from one another. Teams are effective problem-solving tools, and can make a big difference in the way our employees feel about their jobs because they provide a sense of purpose, motivation, and fulfillment. Just remember that we have made some generalizations here. But individuals differ, and not everything will work for everyone. As you gain experience as a supervisor you will be able to see these differences, and make adaptations when necessary. The most important role that you can play as a supervisor is to create the work environment in which these teams can work successfully.

Figures 3.11 and 3.12 contain some sample exercises that can be used to get employees accustomed to working together. They are good icebreakers to the process, as they are not about a specific issue. Using them gives the supervisor an opportunity to watch how the employees interact among one another. This is useful information to have for situations where you need to select people to be on a work team.

Figure 3.10 Exercise: Team Objective to Establish Project

Objective: We want all team members to have a chance to imagine their ideal project.

What you need: Participants and a flip chart and markers, or a blackboard and chalk, paper and pencils

Procedure: Tell the team members that you have just received a call from the Library Director that the Library has been given an anonymous donation of $1,000,000.

Give each team member a piece of paper and a pencil and two minutes. In those two minutes, tell them that they are to write down their own "wish list" for the library.

Next, ask each member to share their top priority wish with the rest of the team. Write down these choices on the flip chart.

Then, as a team, discuss the individual priority wishes, and attempt to bring the team to a consensus on one item.

Follow-up Discussion Questions:
1. If the team's top priority is really important, is it possible to find the necessary funding to accomplish it (city funding, a capital campaign, a grant)?

2. How forcefully did each team member express their view on the priority items? Why?

3. Did team members alter their own wish list when they heard what was on the wish lists of others?

Figure 3.11   Exercise: Team Objective to Establish Cooperation

Objective: To establish a positive climate and spirit of cooperation among team members

Materials Needed: Flip chart and markers

Process: Ask group members to spend two minutes developing a mental image of what their work situation at the library would ideally be like a year from now.

Then ask everyone to describe their vision. Limit the comments to no more than two minutes per person. Post their descriptions on a flip chart.

Divide the team into subgroups. Have them split the descriptions, and then work on developing an action plan listing all of the issues that would come under the group's control to accomplish the overall vision. (10–15 minutes)

Then, have each subgroup report their action plans out to the rest of the group.

Follow-up Questions:
1.   How feasible are the overall plans?

2.   What factors may prevent the library from being successful? How can we overcome these barriers?

3.   How often do we need to review this progress toward the goal to see that it will be accomplished?

Figure 3.12   Exercise: Team Objective to Confront Challenges

Objective: To obtain several possible solutions or suggestions for the participants' current challenges or problems.

Materials required: Paper, pencils

Procedure: Note: The team members should be sitting around a table or in a circle to make this work best.

Ask each person to think about a current job-related problem or concern.

Each person should write his or her problem on a piece of paper. After allowing a few minutes for the participants to think about and write down their problems, ask each person to pass his or her sheet to the right. That person then reads the problem just received and jots down the first thought(s) that come to mind for addressing the problem.

Rotate the papers every minute. Keep the process going until each person gets his or her own paper back.

Follow-up questions for discussion:

1.   Did anyone discover any novel solutions to a problem that had not been previously considered?

2.   Can you see any value in trying to implement these suggestions?

3.   Do some of these suggestions trigger other ideas or solutions for you?

4.   What lesson does this exercise teach us about reaching out to others for assistance? About the synergy that comes from teamwork?

4 DIRECTING ONGOING STAFF TRAINING

None of the decisions that you make as a supervisor will be as important as the ones that you make regarding staff. This starts with selecting the right people to do the particular job that you have in mind, and continues with their orientation and training so that they will be able to perform capably in your library. Because of the changing nature of our field, training is an ongoing activity. As a supervisor, you are in a good place to observe behaviors and processes and evaluate them. You will find that often this will be the first step in deciding what types of training are needed in your library.

START NEW EMPLOYEES OUT RIGHT! HOLD ORIENTATION SESSIONS

The orientation process provides all new employees with a broad perspective on the library system that they have just joined. It discusses how the department in which they will work fits into the overall library as a whole and how the library fits into the community. If you think back to the days when you were a "new hire," you can probably remember some of the insecurities and concerns you had concerning your new situation. You may remember asking yourself all sorts of questions. For example, if the library is to open at 10 a.m., but you were told to report at 9 a.m., how do you get in? Or maybe it was when will I know my schedule for the next week, or month? You may also remember feeling like the outsider that you were until you joined the staff. Immediately involving new personnel in an orientation program gives them a positive feeling of belonging and creates an excitement about working in your library. While doing a thorough orientation does take time, the benefits of to the employer as well as to the employee are well worth the effort. This process gives the library, through its supervisors and administration, the ability to communicate the library's goals and make performance expectations very clear to everyone. It is unreasonable to expect people to do a job unless we tell them what it is! Furthermore, there is real value realized when employees' anxieties are eased and they can begin to become a part of the library and know whom they can go to with questions. The orientation process also makes it imperative that the library has its policies and procedures written down. This is the only way to ensure that everyone is told not only the same thing, but also the correct information.

While most libraries have similar goals and missions, every library *is* just a little bit different. Like other organizations, it is a composite of its people, its procedures, and its services. Sometimes, many of the subtle differences are found out only by trial and error simply because we are so used to doing things that they are second nature to us and we don't think about them. This may cause some further anxieties and delays in a new employee adapting to their new situation, and just gives us one more good reason to write down information. Most libraries have few staff to spare, and if the library is filling a vacancy with this new employee, chances are that you will need the new hire to "hit the ground running." Although new employees may have acquired library skills and experience elsewhere, they still need to know your library's way of doing things. It is a good idea to either pair newcomers with a seasoned employee or with you so that they get an immediate understanding of the culture in which they are expected to work. Your role as supervisor is to be alert and to cue new hires in about local practices and "office politics." While we are not suggesting that the supervisor "gossip," we do feel that it is important that new employees are coached on the nuances of the library and not made to stand alone. A simple example may be that the new person sees an area of the library that needs some cleaning, so they decide to tell the cleaning service to do it. Little did they know that the cleaning service employees are a little temperamental, and do not want to take "orders" from everyone on staff. They only want to hear it from their contact person. It seems trivial, but this and other instances might cause new employees to develop some hard feelings with others on the staff without even knowing what they did. It is important that we remember that proper orientation can determine how quickly a newly hired person can be productive and made to feel a part of the team.

POINTS TO COVER IN A FORMAL ORIENTATION PROCESS

- The mission of your library
- The philosophy of service in your library
- Organizational policies and practices
- Review of organizational chart; chain of command
- Review of job description, functions, and responsibilities
- Review of performance expectations, criteria and standards, and evaluation
- Outline of what you expect from the employee in regard to productivity, attitude, reliability, initiative, personal appearance
- Outline conditions of employment, including the probationary period, punctuality, attendance, conduct, and other appropriate procedures
- Explain safety and emergency procedures
- Opportunities for personal development
- Opportunities/process for advancement
- Tour of the physical facility
- Introduction to other staff members
- Introduction to Board, friends, and other community leaders as appropriate
- Pay/fringe benefits that may be handled by the library's human resource department, and additionally by union representatives, depending on the particular situation
- Personnel policies and practices (Sick, Vacation, and Bereavement Days, Dress Code)
- "Housekeeping"—parking, lockers, staff amenities, keys

There are formal orientations and informal orientations. Both are important activities and they are different experiences. It is appropriate to conduct both types of the process to acclimate the employees to the library.

On the Job Q & A

Q: What should I do when a staff member makes a mistake?

A: Turn the mistake into a learning experience. Don't criticize, but deal with the person in a constructive way. Help them focus on the reason for their error, and give them advice on how to avoid similar problems in the future.

POINTS TO COVER DURING INFORMAL ORIENTATION

The following are items that the supervisor should do on a one-to-one basis to get employees accustomed to the practices of your library. In addition to providing the new employee with some needed information, it is the start of the building relationship that must be developed between the employee and you, the supervisor.

- Staff amenities (where in the building to eat lunch, park a car, get into the building before posted opening time, etc.)
- Staff relationships (how are birthdays, sunshine funds, etc., handled at the library?).
- Networking with other staff members and the community, if appropriate
- Let people know that mistakes are inevitable, and that all questions are important and welcomed. Let them know that you are there to help them and correct them if necessary so that they can avoid future mistakes.
- Let them know if there is a particular time of day or day of the week that is very busy for you. This will let them know that you are not avoiding them, but that there is something else that has to be a priority at these identified times.
- Check in with the new employees regularly so that they feel comfortable with you. This will show them that you are available to them so that the can voice their concerns.
- Don't be openly critical about current employees at any time, but especially to new employees. If their job will demand interaction with other employees, be positive and tell them which employees will be helpful to them, rather than telling them which ones to avoid. If there is information that you need to give or corrective action needs to be taken, do so in private with the employee—away from all other staff and the public!
- New workers are often reluctant to seek out the "boss." Let them know that you welcome talking with them.
- Offer encouragement as people are learning their job. This will give them the assurance that they are doing what you expect of them. It will also keep them motivated so that they will continue to do a good job.
- Always be patient; again, remember what it was like for you to be "new."

- Lose the attitude of "this is how we did it in my day when I was a new employee." Things change for a reason. Your positive attitude will be a much better model for the employee than your recollections of days gone by.

EXPECTATIONS OF THE LIBRARY DIRECTOR

The idea of *the boss,* in this case the Library Director, but really it is the same at any job, is intimidating to some people. Who is this person? What is this person like? How does he or she "run" (read, rule) the library? In actuality, rather than fear the management, employees have every right to have expectations of them. Library Directors also have jobs, and unless they do them, the rest of the staff is not able to proceed with these. While time may not permit the Library Director to conduct the orientation, it is absolutely essential that he or she participate and share their philosophies about libraries as well as welcoming the new comers.

Following is a list of expectations that the staff and especially supervisors can reasonably expect from a Library Director. If wise, the Director will share this information during the orientation process.

- The Director must share the vision for the library. If only the Director knows the vision, the staff will not be able to help the library reach it.
- The Director has the responsibility of creating a risk-taking environment. New opportunities are the result of risk-taking, also known as leadership.
- In the best situations, the Director makes a provision of an environment that gives the staff the freedom to fail, even while it is encouraging achievement. While perfection is nice, recognizing that everyone is human, and that humans make mistakes, will go a lot further in developing staff.
- The Director works along with the Board and the staff to set goals and objectives for the library. They do not perform this function in a vacuum.
- Directors must practice communication that conveys expectations, removes barriers, and allows for feedback from the staff.

- The Director has a responsibility to provide recognition and rewards for achievers.

EXPECTATIONS OF THE SUPERVISOR FROM THE LIBRARY DIRECTOR

Likewise, the Director has the right to expect certain performance benchmarks from his or her supervisors and have the ability to hold them accountable for them. These expectations must also be clearly communicated to the staff members so that they have an understanding of what it is that supervisors do. In addition to meeting performance standards, a good supervisor will:

- Be willing to do other duties as assigned
- Go beyond what is expected
- Be a model
- Reinforce good service among staff members
- Be enthusiastic
- Be creative

Good management is central to the library's survival. The supervisor who goes above and beyond will meet this challenge.

On the Job Q & A

Q: How can I influence employee retention?

A: Start by carefully assessing the job and applicant before hiring. Provide adequate training. Clarify the library and department goals. Offer clear, consistent instructions. Provide helpful feedback.

Figure 4.1   Sample: Orientation Outline for New Employees

The following is a sample basic outline for an orientation program for new employees. It should be adapted with the particular needs of your library in mind.

Anytown's Public Library Training Traditions

A. Welcome

Thank the person/group for choosing to work for the Anytown Library.

Your remarks should convey your pride in the library.

The Director should give a welcome and overview. Then the program can be turned over to a supervisor or other individual who is conducting the orientation program.

B. Library's History

A brief overview (if there is a written document, this is even better) provides newcomers with a sense of how the library is positioned within the community.

C. Library's Mission and Goals

A written copy of the library's strategic plan should be provided; current practices and future plans should be addressed.

The library should have clearly stated written standards and distribute these as well at this time.

D. Operational Procedures and Policies

A written copy of all policies and procedures should be provided.

Give everyone an overview of the ongoing operations, and how the job they will do relates to the other jobs in the library. Explain performance standards.

Also, this is a good time to provide an overview of future plans.

E. Library's Philosophy

This gives the library administration opportunity to emphasize some of the values that are most important to your particular library.

Examples: Customer service is key—make people feel that they are valuable.

We expect quality—put the emphasis on doing your job right.

We are a team—good library service is everyone's job.

F. Professional Development

Fully explain ongoing onsite training as well as all opportunities for training and further education that may be available. Encourage full participation and the importance of sharing what the employee has learned at a workshop/seminar with other employees.

Let the employee know if the library will cover their membership dues for any professional organization. At the very least, the library should encourage all professionals to join.

G. Networking Opportunities

Networking opportunities may occur within the structure of the library system, the city, or through other organizations such as the Chamber of Commerce. The emphasis should be on how this might impact the quality of the job/library service. Encouragement for the library staff to meet and talk with community members is a very important aspect of knowing one's community, which will result in better library service.

ON-THE-JOB TRAINING

Whether the situation is that there are new employees, new equipment, or revised procedures, providing on-the-job training is a necessary part of every supervisor's job. This is training that goes beyond the basic introductory orientation and this is especially true because of the nature of our library work. We always want to present our best face to the public. Learning, gaining experience from performing tasks or observing others, then practicing, are helpful ways to have employees develop.

Failure to train properly can have devastating consequences for a library. Depending on the nature of the information that should be communicated during the sessions, lack of training can result in poor performance, low productivity, the need for increased supervision, high employee turnover, and discipline and motivation problems in the workplace, among others. Therefore, ongoing staff development must be seen as a priority.

Sometimes the training will be on the organization's philosophy. Or it may be on new technologies or changes in policies and procedures. It is important to also consider training on not only how to do a job, but also *why* the job is important to the library. This is true even when employees come to us with experience or for employees who have been with the library for a long time. It is often necessary that we provide some training so that they can learn the way things are done in our library or the *new* way to complete a task. Sometimes, this is a relatively easy process and employees are eager to have new opportunities to learn. At other times, it may be frustrating for supervisors. It is often difficult for people to discard their previous habits and to learn another way to do something. One of the greatest shortcomings of service providers is the tendency to continue to perform tasks in a way that is comfortable for the staff members, even when the patrons' needs may indicate that a different approach would be better. If our staff members are going to be effective, they must add new behaviors to their repertoires. I also realize that it also is difficult to accept that you are going to be spending some time on training while there does not seem to be enough time to do everything right now! However, it is really important that you plan these activities during work time and have as many people as possible participate. After all, if people are on "work time," they should be attentive to what is happening. In the long run, you will find that training is actually a time saver.

Training programs need to take into account both individual worker's development needs and the library's goal-directed needs.

It is very likely that you will need to train individuals in the context of their current work as well as to teach them how to offer innovative services. You will also need to make some decisions if the same training will be offered to both professional and support staff, or if it should be different. You will also be required to make decisions on when to include volunteers in the training loop. Again, the relevance to your particular library is what will be the guiding factor in the development of the training programs. Other factors that you will need to consider as you design the training for your library, include will the decision if the training is going to be best accomplished on a one-to-one basis, or if group training is the better option. One of the things to take into consideration is that when you offer sessions for groups, you will find that employees become a support system for one another. Helpful hints and reminders are more likely to be passed around. Training that is well designed will bring employees up to speed quickly, resulting in a cost-efficient, effective experience for everyone. This is teamwork at its best.

While informational speakers and lecture opportunities may be appropriate with some topics, it is often more important that we offer "hands-on" opportunities. The best way to train people to do jobs is to actively go through the actual motions that are required to perform the task. Reinforcement, rehearsal, and explanation are all components of this type of job training. A bulleted handout is also a handy reinforcement tool. While training at work may not be as exciting an opportunity as going to an outside workshop, this type of training may provide even more essential skill development opportunities. Furthermore, it must be remembered that training does not end when instruction does. The supervisor who supports the staff in what they have been taught in order to make a long-term difference must evaluate progress and oversee implementation.

DESIGNING AN ENVIRONMENT FOR LEARNING

A good training outline is essential, but it can be, an ineffective tool if the supervisor has not taken the time to create an atmosphere at work where people are eager to learn. Here are some ideas on how a supervisor can help create a learning environment for their employees.

On the Job Q & A

Q: I have several older employees who are reluctant to learn new technological innovations, and I really need them to know how to do these things. How do I know if they are intimidated or just plain stubborn? What should I do?

A: It is important that you explain to the employees that these technological changes are here to stay, and it is important that they learn them. I would schedule some staff training when the library is closed, even if it means that the individuals will have to be paid extra or have time off. That way everyone can concentrate on learning the new processes. I would also try to introduce some fun into the training, with friendly competition and small rewards, if the entire department needs training. If there are only one or two who are hesitant, one-to-one training works best. In any case, it is critical that you are patient and not condescending.

- Make sure that the goal leaves room for "passion, commitment, and a sense of ownership." Of course we want those we employ to help the library achieve its goals and mission. However, a successful a manager knows that it is important that there is enough room to let people "shape" the goal according to their own personal interests. The supervisor can be instrumental in this process by assigning the right person for the right task.
- Encourage self-directed learning. Don't dictate what people must learn unless it is absolutely essential in order to complete their job. Rather, provide them with learning opportunities and they will gravitate to those where they already have a basic interest.
- Promote learning by cross-training. Many projects are best served by mixing people from different functional specialties so that different views and perspectives are brought to the table. The supervisor makes sure that people have enough time to spend together, and in a qualitative way. This is important because it gets people thinking about what is best for the library as a whole, rather than from one department's or person's perspective.
- Ask questions. When the supervisor illustrates that it is important to ask questions, the message is what is important is learning as opposed to knowing. This encourages people to ask questions, formulate ideas, and even brainstorm out loud until they find the best way to get the desired result.
- View mistakes as learning opportunities. Review what works and what does not work. Ask for ideas on how to fix the situation from the group without making it personal or pointing out who made the error. The synergy of group brainstorming is much greater than individual thinking. Use it wisely.
- Remember that the more often we hear, see, and do things, and the easier that they can be related to things we already know, the more likely we will be able to learn new procedures and techniques. Repetition is important.

TRAINING GOALS

Every well-run program knows its purpose and goals. We advise you to think about these as you recommend particular areas of training. Some sample goals may include but are not limited to the following:

- Ensure that the staff knows and understands the library's policies and procedures.
- Teaches appropriate skills to implement the policies and procedures.
- Provides a means for ongoing discussion about common problem situations.
- Develops skills for a particular time and place.

Remember, participants must know what the goal is before the training begins. They must be told what specific behaviors that they are expected to achieve, and then, they must be given the opportunity to do them. Understanding the purpose will go a long way in creating an environment that is conducive to adult learning.

POINTS TO CONSIDER FOR ON-THE-JOB TRAINING

These are some important tips to keep in mind as you proceed to develop training workshops at your library.

- Teach simple tasks first
- Break down each task to basic components
- Teach only correct procedures
- Keep training cycles short
- Reinforce the training with practice; skills are developed with repetition
- Motivate, then reward the trainees
- Repeat until you are sure that your employees understand

TRAINING NEEDS FOR SUPERVISORS TO IDENTIFY

Supervisors will be able to identify the training needs of their libraries by paying attention to what is happening on a day-to-day basis and listening to their employees. You will then be able to make the decision on whether this is training that can be offered within your library by someone who is already on staff, or if you will need to send staff to outside workshops as funds allow. The author recommends a look at her earlier book, *Successful Staff Development,* (New York: Neal-Schuman, 1995) for an in-depth look at this topic. Remember that every library is different, and designing programs that are specific to your individual library's needs is an important task that a supervisor should undertake. Also, if you can identify learning opportunities as more than just learning how to complete tasks, you are helping employees see the broader picture of library service and helping them develop a work ethic. Having representation from different departments will also help with this, and teamwork is a nice result. All staff members must come to understand that the opportunity is there to explain that what we do today, no matter what the task may be, is worth it to upgrade the quality of our service for the long run.

However, by their nature, libraries of all kinds and sizes have similarities. The following is a list of some topic areas that we have found to be needed almost universally in libraries. You may find opportunities to send staff to programs that address these that may be offered on a regional or state level. Or, you may feel that there are some differences with your particular experience, and your staff will be better served if the program is tailored to the needs of your particular library. The following is a list of common themes for training within libraries.

UNIVERSAL LIBRARY TRAINING THEMES

- How to handle patron complaints
- How to handle difficult patrons
- Good telephone techniques
- De-escalating conflict (between staff, or staff/patrons)
- Problem-solving/developing alternate solutions
- Using informed judgment
- Using specific parts of collection, or new formats/sources
- Customer Service techniques
- Being a good team player
- When to involve law enforcement personnel

The use of the form in Figure 4.2 is a tool that will assist you in making decisions about the quantity and the direction that training should take for your staff.

Figure 4.2 Sample: Employee Training Questionnaire

Instructions: Please read the list of training areas. Circle Yes if you believe you need more training in those skills. Circle No if you feel that no training is needed in that area.

1. How to more effectively manage my time	Yes	No
2. How to handle stress on the job	Yes	No
3. How to improve written communication skills	Yes	No
4. How to improve oral communications skills	Yes	No
5. How to improve listening skills	Yes	No
6. How to improve personal productivity	Yes	No
7. How to improve customer relations skills	Yes	No
8. How to improve computer skills	Yes	No
9. How to improve interpersonal relations skills	Yes	No
10. How to improve safety/security	Yes	No

ASSESSING LEARNING NEEDS AND DESIGNING THE TRAINING PROGRAM

There are two main reasons that you want to take the time to do an assessment of learning needs within your library. The first is so that you can be sure that you are using your resources most efficiently and appropriately. The second reason revolves around motivation. In either case, the result you are looking for is a clear recognition that a goal can be achieved only after some training has been implemented. You will want to examine a problem in service delivery that is occurring. Or you may heed suggestions from employees, or you may be aware that there are changes on the way for your automated system. All of these can be methods of assessing a need for a training program.

The design of the training program depends on what objectives are to be met and what resources are available. Training can be special workshops for groups, individualized programmed instruction, and instruction through an audiovisual media, lab training sessions, or conference going. Lectures, panel discussions, case studies, demonstrations, role-playing or other simulations are all proven methods of training. Sometimes "passive" learning is appropriate. Individuals can learn from reading, watching films, listening to taped lectures/directions. Other training may require the learner's active participation and involvement. Some methods are better suited for some activities than others, so part of the design task is to determine which type of session to hold and what teaching strategies to use. And we should also remember that people learn differently. Some require a hands-on approach, others may need graphics or visuals, and still others would prefer to proceed at their own pace. If you know your employees, these differences in learning styles will become clear.

Finally, the design must take into consideration the adult learner's motivation. You are requiring people to participate in this training. This creates a very different atmosphere than the formal education process where someone has made a conscious decision to take classes. Motivation may come in the form of convincing people that the training will simply help them to perform a job well. Or it may be in the form of a financial reward, or a promotion. Everyone will need to recognize the importance of this training to his or her own job function. As the supervisor, you should help your employees recognize that the skills and the knowledge they are gaining are important for their continued job success. You reinforce this by giving them the opportunity to use their new knowledge. Without taking motivation into consideration, it is likely that you will have set up a program that will cause "grumbles" and be considered a waste of time.

On the Job Q & A

Q: What if I have a staff member who has been at the library for a while, but I feel that they do not know how to do their job?

A: Train them! One of the largest responsibilities that a manager has is to teach others skills and model behaviors so that they can develop on their job.

QUESTIONS SUPERVISORS SHOULD CONSIDER ABOUT EMPLOYEE LEARNING

As you go about designing enrichment learning activities, there are some points that must be understood before you proceed. Are staff members willing to learn? If not, why not? What can you do about it? Yes, you can make training mandatory, but is that the best way? People may attend but will they pay attention, or even listen? It is important that you ask for their assistance in designing the training, because then they will already be predisposed to it. It is also important that employees see the link between the current practices and results and new practices and results. If the employees can see the differences and the benefits, then you are also able to overcome a barrier to progress.

IMPLEMENTING THE SKILLS FROM TRAINING—THE SUPERVISOR'S ROLE

The next chapter will discuss more fully the supervisor's role as a coach. For training purposes, however, coaching and mentoring in many ways are extension opportunities of the training that we have provided for our employees. These relationships are based on providing employees with guidance on when and how to employ particular skills. It is a way of providing continued feedback, or sharing frustrations and successes. Coaching is a support system, and clearly within the purview of the supervisor's responsibilities. The supervisor should realize that sometimes there are awkward periods when people are employing new skills or using some new resources or tools. They, in fact, may work slower and inefficiently for a while until they have a complete grasp of the new process. Coaching is encouraging behavior on the part of the supervisor and the way that a supervisor can reinforce the new skills and oversee the behavior changes that are necessary from their employees.

EVALUATING TRAINING

Once the training program is completed, it is important that the supervisor take the time to evaluate the effectiveness of the program. The evaluation process provides the means by which we judge the success of the training process.

This is important not only to adjust and change the actual training process if necessary, but also to determine whether the employees have benefited from the progress. You will want to evaluate the gain in knowledge or skills. While it is not usual to have written "tests" in the workplace for this type of training, performance tests are common. The end result of your evaluation is to determine if the participants have gained the knowledge/skills that you wanted them to have and if they are using them in a practical manner.

Training programs fail when they do not provide the participants the opportunity to practice what they have learned. And, practice without feedback may only serve to make individuals more proficient in their mistakes, so it is crucial for the supervisor to provide it. The feedback must be timely, descriptive, and very specific in order to be effective. Evaluating behavior changes is a supervisor's responsibility and employees will appreciate this if it is constructive. You do not want to make your evaluation process threatening. One of the best ways that you will evaluate as a supervisor is by observing what principles the employees are using in practice. You will then be able to give the appropriate feedback, and take corrective actions if necessary. And finally, your evaluation process is important because you will also want to know what the impact of the training is on the library and its organizational needs. These efforts will help you plan and deliver further training opportunities. In addition to doing the evaluations and providing the feedback to our employees, it is the supervisor's responsibility to recognize achievements. Positive reinforcement, good verbal "pats on the back," and small rewards go a long way to cementing the relationship between supervisors and their employees. You will want to reward progress, not just the final results.

TRAINING TIPS TO USE IN ALL PROGRAMS

- Put employees at ease
- Be realistic with expectations
- Explain the "why"—relate the task at hand to the bigger picture and how it fits in
- Find out what the person already knows and respect their knowledge
- Explain any vocabulary or "buzz" words that may be unfamiliar
- Demonstrate slowly; repeat as needed
- Allow employees practice time
- Review for quality and productivity

The focus of all staff development and training should ultimately be the patron or customer. Staff members must learn that patrons expect us to be reliable; we must provide what is promised dependably and accurately. We must be responsive to their needs and act promptly to meet them. They want the assurance that they are dealing with a knowledgeable staff, and that the equipment that they need to use works. And most of all, patrons want us to have empathy and show a degree of caring and attention to them.

CONTINUING EDUCATION AND PROFESSIONAL CONFERENCES

In addition to the training that you are providing at your library, it makes good sense to have employees attend sessions outside of the library as well. Many state and regional library associations offer free or low-cost opportunities for continuing education. It is important that staff members have the opportunity to attend these. Not only will they come back to the library with new skills, they will also have had the opportunity to talk with their peers in other parts of the state. It is reassuring to hear that others have some of the same problems that you have, and helpful to hear what solutions they have devised to deal with them. Meetings of the state association and of the American Library Association also serve this purpose. It is well worth it to find the funds to send employees to these types of meetings. If your budget does not provide for them, consider asking the Friends of the Library to assist you with this. It may be that everyone cannot attend every year, but think of a fair way of rotating the ability to attend these meetings, or doing a special drawing as a way to accomplish getting people there. And, it is always advisable that supervisors attend those meetings and workshops that are appropriate for their jobs. Also, in this electronic age, consider teleconferences. Participation in this type of learning activity may indeed be more cost effective than sending staff out of state.

We should also not overlook training opportunities that are offered right within our own communities. The Chamber of Commerce is a good source (and often a provider) of this type of experience. Staff members meet others within the community and learn new skills. An example of this is "The Leadership Challenge" that many Chambers offer. This provides a varied curriculum usually over the course of several months to inform people of who's who in the community, how to get things done, how government works, etc. Participants are put to work on a project, and the program does what its name implies. It "grooms" new leaders for the community. Librarians have tremendous skills to offer and this is a good way of polishing them and letting them be known by others.

The added advantage is that they are then able to inform others about what they do, and what is new at the library. This is a tremendous networking opportunity that has multiple benefits. The human resources department of the city where you work, or the local school system may also welcome your staff to training sessions that they have planned. It is worth checking them out. We promote our libraries as being institutions of "lifelong learning." We should take our own advice!

5 MENTORING AND COACHING STAFF

Libraries are labor-intensive organizations. In most cases, better than 60 percent of our budgets are spent on staff salaries. Therefore, it makes sense that the most important decisions that supervisors make are in the human development area. And, because libraries are networks of intersecting components, every job that we have is a building block for the system as a whole.

Coaching and mentoring in the workplace are very important tools for the supervisor. It is a management style that moves the supervisor away from the directive style in which he or she would give the orders and expect the staff then to carry them out. Coaching and mentoring embrace a style that is much more flexible in its approach. It is one that has the supervisor involved on a personal level with the staff members. This technique is rooted in a continuous learning process for both the supervisor and the employee. There are very definite benefits for the supervisor who is a coach. Managers who use these methods achieve the professional satisfaction of seeing their managerial talent. Coaches who delegate their responsibilities and genuinely challenge their employees to better themselves, grow their staff members' skills, and make them more self-sufficient and productive workers are better supervisors. Results-oriented coaches will have the knowledge that they inspired people to perform at higher levels than they would have otherwise if left on their own. Employees who experience job satisfaction are more likely to stay employed at your library as well. Good management creates an environment that makes people, especially those who are self-motivated and want career growth, want to work for you.

Coaching and mentoring are essentially about teaching. Both are action-oriented approaches to managing employee performance. Is there a difference between coaching and mentoring? Essentially, the coach is usually the supervisor who has several employees to oversee and form into a team. Supervisors may indeed also be mentors, pay special attention to an individual employee to help them develop professionally. However, mentors might also be other employees who take a newcomer under his or her wing. The mentor is a role model. A mentor is often someone who can give advice and offers helpful problem-solving hints and ways to overcome obstacles based on their own experiences, especially in that particular workplace. Their advice and hints are based on real-life situations. They are genuine insights and the goal is to share these real lessons learned from both mistakes as well as successes. Mentoring, by definition, is a way to learn from observation of others. The person becomes involved with the mentor, and the mentor inspires trust and challenges their performance. They provide clarification of expectations, and affirmation of good performance. The relationship must always be built on credibility and trust.

In effect, what both mentoring and coaching do is to take the traditional managerial model of planning, implementing, and evaluating and controlling, utilize them, and then focus more on maximizing individual performance. The supervisor's goal will be to expand employees' knowledge about their job, and their skills. This, in effect, is the application of this knowledge into performing a task. Teaching is more than imparting facts; it is about stimulating people to want to learn. And, as a coach, your predominant mission is always to broaden your own competencies along with your employees'. In many ways, being a mentor or a coach does not require you have other skills in addition to the ones that were discussed in earlier chapters. It is simply a matter of implementing them. Mentoring and coaching require that you lead by example and maintain very high ethical standards. It means that you know when you can delegate important responsibilities; this, in itself, is the best evidence that you believe in your employees' talents and abilities. However, although you give can employees latitude, you will not cut them adrift. You will need to pay close attention to them! Listen to them and freely communicate with your staff. And most important of all, treat each and every one of your employees as individuals with distinct personalities and unique competencies. Respect fosters respect, and the development of trust. The ethical standard that you set as the supervisor, in both your words and your deeds, sets the overall tone for your department.

How does coaching/mentoring differ from ongoing staff development? In one sense it is a part of that overall process. However, the coaching and mentoring process usually focuses on a particular result, rather than the more general process of continuing education. Coaching/mentoring is about paying attention to people. It requires that the coach is aware of precisely what needs to be accomplished, and what resources, both personnel and financial, that you have to work with. It requires you know what positive outcomes that you want your staff to achieve. But as the supervisor/coach you must also be aware that things don't always go as planned, and that some people work at different paces and in different ways. You will discover that some employees will need more from you than others. That's okay; an important part of the supervisor's job is to know which employees need that little extra from you, and which ones can work better on their own. And, it requires that you are there—not in your office, or off the grounds, but there where there is implementation of tasks. Sometimes, you will walk that fine line between offering support and encouragement and pushing a bit. If you are successful, you will be able to get the most from your employees by understanding them. You will solve problems without being sidetracked. And your department will have achieved some positive results toward the library's mission. As with all work, it is crucial that the process of coaching or mentoring be monitored and the relationship evaluated.

Other potential sources of help about the role of coaches and mentors can often be found in professional associations, through various books and periodicals. Mentoring can also be a reciprocal experience rather than a top-down one from supervisor to employee. Senior staff members who are feeling a little out of date should take advantage of both the knowledge and the enthusiasm that younger co-workers bring to the library. We have seen this especially in the area of technology. Newcomers to the library have grown up with it while those of us who have been at it for a while can benefit from their savvy.

A MENTOR'S SCRIPT

Mentoring is not a new idea. Some of the earliest mentions of the process of mentoring goes back to Homer when Odysseus needs a mentor to guide him while he is on his journey. The job of mentoring means that you as an individual will be passing on wisdom of your experience to someone who will benefit from it. This professional relationship is established when you believe that something significant and positive for the library will result. Mentoring is an evolving relationship. As you move forward and make progress, you will add to the relationship. Mentoring is not an easy process. It requires patience and sincere commitment on the part of both parties. And, undoubtedly, there will be setbacks. That's okay, as long as you recognize what caused them, and together come up with a way to continue on. But if you take the time to get to know one another and take a slow, determined approach, the rewards will be significant. I have mentioned that mentoring is a relationship, and the "seasoned" employee does learn quite a bit from the newcomer. Through the use of feed-

---

On the Job Q & A

Q: How do I support a staff member?

A: There are several different ways, and you will be the best judge of which technique to use in a given situation. Some examples are recognition and praise for the staff member, especially in a public venue. You can also appeal to people's egos by asking for their input. Or you can outline in a rational, logical manner reasons why something must be done, even though the staff member may not agree with it. Most off all, you can inspire your staff with your own enthusiasm.

back, and open-ended questioning, a mentor can determine if he or she is being effective. This is important because it keeps the supervisor motivated to reach deeper into themselves so that they will be able to come up with techniques and solutions that their protégé can then use. Every employee at some point in his or her career requires a guiding hand of some kind on the job. Some employees may even want to have more than one mentor. For example, the may want to model their reference interview skills after one employee, and their storytelling skills after another.

Be flexible and encourage employees to seek out the experts for assistance as well as yourself.

BENEFITS OF PROVIDING MENTORING

- Articulate employees
- Employees who are self-aware
- Skilled employees
- Resilient employees
- Focused employees
- Positive employees
- Trustworthy and willing to trust others
- Sensitive and more open to differences of opinion
- Better problem solvers
- Better able to recognize opportunities and seize them
- Stronger work teams

WHAT IS THE SUPERVISOR'S ROLE?

Your supervisory role makes it imperative that you be a model to all employees. This is the start of the coaching relationship. All employees must be made to understand that you know how to do their job, and face the challenges that may be presented. They must also begin to trust that you will do exactly what you tell them what you are going to do, and when, and then they need to see you perform. While everyone's style is different, if you are enthusiastic and have passion about your work, your attitude will begin to trickle down to others.

What are the characteristics of being a good supervisor or coach? Rule number one is to exhibit professionalism at all times.

On the Job Q & A

Q: Help! One of our book shelvers has applied for a job in the technical services department, which I supervise. She's very nice and has worked here for years. BUT... she's never used a computer. She doesn't even know how to play solitaire. I'd like to give her a chance (it would be a nice raise for her), since she knows everything else required for the job, but I don't know how to tell her she needs training. Can you help me out?

A: Use the written job description when you speak with her. This will let her know that you are not singling her out, but rather that anyone who is hired for the position must be able to use a computer. Also, ask her if she is willing to learn the computer. You may have training in place for this sort of thing, but if not, almost every adult education program or community college offers beginning computer training. If your library has a program that helps cover tuition for these programs, share the info. Give her the chance, but also provide support and follow-up.

Professionalism includes the attributes of honesty and integrity. You must be truthful, open, and upfront at all times. And you must insist that everyone who works for you is too. Your personal ethics are perhaps the most significant force that will shape your career, and your life. The second attribute is to be always open to learning. You must want to acquire new skills and knowledge and you should demonstrate initiative and creativity. Thirdly, you must project resilience. The process of coaching anticipates and welcomes change. We all know that change is sometimes difficult for people. However, as a supervisor, you will be expected to take a few "punches" and not fall down. Often these may be at a moment's notice, and may require a shift from your plans. Flexibility is what makes this process work. Next in line is your attitude. It should always emphasize the positive. When all of these attributes are put together, it creates an environment that is harmonious, challenging, and full of opportunities for employees.

The use of a coaching style of management puts the focus on people. There is the understanding that the quality of product/service is clearly a result of this people process. A coach is someone who see things in situations that others can't or don't see. Their insight is what can make the difference in reaching a goal. Coaching is helping people to learn rather than doing the job for them. Good coaching starts by engaging staff members with a discussion that clarifies goals, visions, and ideas. The good coach thinks in terms of people's potential, not just their current performance. The good coach gets everyone on board right away and engages each with their agreement that they want to be challenged and supported in their work. Building consensus becomes the cornerstone for productive work on issues and problems and makes possible decisions, plans, and strategies that everyone can stand behind. The most obvious benefit to the supervisor is that if coaching is done well, then the supervisor will have the time to deal with the overarching responsibilities of his or her job, rather than standing over someone's shoulder and watching them as they perform their work. People who have been coached and then given tasks to do independently then feel respected and responsible. They achieve personal development while simultaneously the work gets done.

CHARACTERISTICS OF A GREAT COACH

Don't be surprised—the characteristics that we mentioned in Chapter 2 that define a good supervisor *also* define a good coach. First and foremost, a coach must have the ability to inspire. They do this by helping people recognize possibilities within themselves and their circumstances. They then help them take the steps that will turn these possibilities into actions. The second characteristic that distinguishes a good coach is their ability to set higher standards, for themselves and others. Good coaches recognize that it is not acceptable to just get by; they are always striving to do just a little bit better. Coaches who hold themselves to the highest standards of honesty and integrity, because these are values that are important to them, meet the third characteristic that sets them apart from others. These characteristics distinguish a genuine commitment to success that puts the good of the organization above other considerations. The fourth characteristic is being able to call upon an individual's inner motivation to get a job rather than on outside pressures or deadlines. This is the ability to get full participation with everyone focused on the task at hand. A good coach does not stop at making a plan; rather he or she makes himself and their team focus on action, on what the next steps must be in order to achieve a goal. And finally, a good coach has the inner desire to help others learn, grow, and achieve. They are very perceptive about what people are currently doing, and what their potential may be. They pay attention to not only what is needed to get a job done today, but also what development is needed over the next few years for their staff members. They recognize it is their job to help someone else succeed. Communicating with employees means getting to know your employees, and this is makes coaching work. In summary, a coach is patient, supportive, interested, a good listener, perceptive, attentive, and aware of what is going on, and self-aware and self-confident. A good coach will pay attention to the short-term goals first, and once these are understood, then, moves on to the long-term goals. It also helps if the coach has the technical expertise and the knowledge to do all of the jobs that he or she supervises. Coaches must support all employees with no exceptions; they cannot "play favorites."

BENEFITS OF COACHING

The practice of coaching offers many benefits to the library as well as to the individuals involved. These include:

- Helps individuals develop a personal vision and goals that are consistent with the library's
- Provides the impetus for the attitudes and actions necessary to reach these goals
- Emphasizes the importance of continuous learning so that knowledge and skills are always growing
- Is results-oriented
- Builds mutual respect
- Emphasizes learning to achieve performance results; performance growth is related to personal growth
- Offers guidance and consistent oversight in overcoming negative personality traits/skill deficits that might impede career growth
- Increases self-awareness, and thus better relationships among co-workers
- Develops networking relationships that also influence career opportunities
- Engages individuals in real dialogue—offers constructive feedback, and welcomes it in return
- Stresses open communication, both written and oral
- Builds confidence and personal satisfaction
- Strengthens problem-solving skills; look at every problem as having a solution
- Understands the importance of self-motivation and commitment to the job and the library
- Coaching is a direct, people-intensive approach. It is results-oriented

As you can see, there are both benefits and obstacles listed here. As the coach, you will help employees and yourself overcome these by gaining confidence in their abilities, by becoming aware of their strengths and their weaknesses, and how they can work with others to balance these out.

WHAT DO COACHES DO

- Provide focus and clear priorities
- Provide clarity and direction
- Develop performance goals
- Source of guidance and advice
- Provide encouragement
- Challenge people to put forth their best effort
- Make suggestions for improvement
- Keep up morale
- Provide training opportunities
- Provide resources
- Remove barriers
- Assist with career and personal development

COACHING AS A CATALYST FOR PRODUCTIVITY

The coach is a catalyst in the arena of job performance. You were hired or promoted to help other employees help themselves, so it is your responsibility to see that they work as productively and effectively as possible. With staff development, you have a planned program of activities. With coaching, you never quite know when the opportunity or the time to act might arise for you to make a difference with an employee's productivity. You have to be prepared to act when you judge that the time is right to teach valuable lessons, because no learning is as effective as situational learning can be. Part of your job as a supervisor is to raise your employees' self-awareness, self-confidence, and thus their self-development. As the coach, you understand the "game" and its "rules" and you put them into play when you need to see results.

There are six main areas into which what we call "coachable" moments might be categorized, three are for positive reinforcement, and three are to take corrective actions. The first one is in looking at jobs that have been well done. It is important to give positive feedback—that verbal "pat on the back" for a job well done. However, it is probably even more important to meet with the individuals who have shown great success or productivity and to analyze what went right. Was it the planning and preparation?

On the Job Q & A

Q: I am so overwhelmed by constant change! Will it ever stop?

A: Change has always been with us and will always be a part of our lives. The trick is to manage it and not let it overwhelm you. **One hint:** Evaluate current activities. Are they relics of the past and no longer needed? If so, eliminate them. Just because it was done so much in the past doesn't make it a good process for now. Be open-minded and embrace change.

Were there particular skills used? What was the attitude, the work ethic, or the overall approach to the job? Were there outside influences that made a difference? How were they able to take advantage of them? Did they make adjustments to their plan to accommodate other influences? It is important to ask these questions because you want this behavior to be repetitive. You must also insist that individuals also take responsibility when things go wrong. If you have created an environment where there is give-and-take, people will own up to their mistakes and learn from them. Or, they may ask you for advice on how to proceed differently on another occasion. If you have taken the time to establish relationships with employees, you will be in a position to understand when there are errors, and employees will come to expect solution-oriented assistance. Feedback, not criticism, must be given when things are not quite right. This is called corrective coaching. It should always be constructive, honest, and succinct. You must talk with your employees about what you believe is the problem, and discuss possible solutions. This coaching action helps individuals understand their success, and it keeps them doing what works. And, a solution to a problem results in taking a mistake and making it have a positive outcome. A simple pattern for dealing with negative situations is to take a moment to review what happened. Extract the lesson from it, and then apply it to another situation. In addition to this issue now becoming positive, as a coach you will have shared a process that employees will be able to apply themselves to another set of circumstances. If you take the attitude that you must seize every opportunity to teach lessons, you will find that you have become an effective coach. After all, the aim of coaching is to better people's skills.

ABOUT MOTIVATION

Your role of supervisor/coach will include the need to "motivate" people. Actually, it is your job to inspire people to motivate themselves because it is entirely up to individuals if they are motivated or not. However, you can use persuasion and influencing skills to encourage employee self-motivation. Employees must adopt the notion that their productivity on the job benefits them. Rewarding good work is a much more effective management tool than threatening punitive measures for bad work. The salary associated with the job motivates some individuals. Or, maybe it's personal satisfaction from a job well done. An essential foundation for motivation is the positive workplace environment that is created by you, the supervisor. Employees have the right to expect fair treatment and understanding. Staff will not commit to an uncommitted manager, so it is important that you motivate yourself as well as others. The amount of energy that you put into your work will be one of the primary indicators to staff about your motivation. Your job will be to know what factors might influence employee performance and do what you can to move them along.

Coaching gives you the ability to tap into the talent and the ability of your staff. It encourages innovation and creativity, and it makes you adaptable with making things happen. If the situation happens to be one that you do not want to see repeated, then it is important to take the time to review what just happened and extract the lesson from it. Then, as the supervisor, you can give some scenarios on how this lesson can then be applied to another set of circumstances.

One of the basic components of creating a motivational environment is the cooperation which you must give to your staff as well as expect from them. It is essential that you are genuine, because forced cheerfulness, or hiding facts, are recognizable through voice tones and body language. Do follow up on suggestions, requests and comments. Inform staff of the use of their ideas, give them credit, and let them know the success rate of their ideas. The coaching and mentoring process encourages employees to look for challenges and for innovative ways of meeting those challenges. Have good reasons for refusing employee requests. Check to make sure that your directions have been understood. Find the root cause of complaints and eradicate them quickly. On the other hand, do not ask for advice unless you respect the potential advisor. You will then be put in a position of using advice that you may find questionable, or, perceived to be ignoring information that you requested. Provide the right resources if you want the right results. If you cooperate by acting on requests, you can bring about major improvements in motivation. Not acting on feedback will de-motivate people. Don't leave people without clear instructions and guidelines to follow. It is important that you find that happy balance between leaving people free to perform as they wish, and encouraging them to meet their goals, proceeding independently, with advice from you. Success encourages employees, so it is important that you keep employees rooted in achievable goals so that they can realize that success.

SOME TOOLS THAT MOTIVATE EMPLOYEES

- A simple thank-you
- Pay raises
- Bonuses
- Promotions
- Work that is worthwhile and interesting
- Positive performance reviews
- Positive feedback
- Recognition
- Opportunity to represent the library
- Opportunity to attend state, regional, or national conferences (with expenses paid)
- Increases in job responsibilities and challenges
- Public acclaim (newsletter article, "employee of the month," etc.)

Once you have successfully raised the motivation levels of your staff, it is important that you remain consistent so that these levels remain raised. Ask yourself the following questions to evaluate your ability as a motivator. If you find that you are not answering these positively, then you need to examine how you are portraying yourself to your employees.

1. I try to persuade and influence staff rather than force them to do what I want.
2. I give my staff my complete information whenever possible.
3. I try to make work fun and enjoyable.
4. I involve people in issues at the earliest possible opportunity.
5. I seek consensus and encourage others to do the same.
6. I work to create a balance between giving people independence and firm control.
7. I ask people to do something in such a way that they are delighted to do it.
8. I give reasons for my actions and for any disagreements with people.
9. I react to failure not by blame but by analysis of what went wrong and solutions for corrections.
10. I make conscious efforts to know those I supervise.

On the Job Q & A

Q: I have begun mentoring the newest staff member and now it appears my attention has made older employees jealous. What should I do?

A: If you know your employees, then you know their strengths. I would suggest that you ask each of the older jealous employees to spend some one-to-one time with the newest employee, perhaps to introduce them to a process/or task. This will make them feel special and appreciated for their skill, and they will also learn a lot by taking the time to teach someone else.

11. I revise work plans in order to remove obstacles for performance.
12. I encourage people too show initiative and to act on it.
13. I look at work assignments as ways to develop people.
14. I pay attention to feedback, and respond appropriately.
15. I thank people, face-to-face, or with handwritten notes.
16. I reward, recognize, and promote within my power when the situation merits it

REACHING SUCCESS

Coaching does take time, and you and your organization will have to make a determination on how much time you will spend on the process in addition to other tasks that you are assigned. However, it is time that is well spent. And it isn't all the time either. Coaching may be cyclical based on projects or situations; or, it may be the ongoing preferred system of management in your library. If so, the administration will provide the reinforcement for you, the supervisor, so that you, in turn, can pass it on to your charges. Remember, our goal is to provide the best quality of service to our patrons, and using the coaching model is a technique that will help us achieve this goal.

Coaching people to take successful action often starts with focusing on some areas where people have not been successful. The coach sees everything, evaluates everything, and considers nothing as inconsequential. However, for a coach to lead a team successfully, they must have the commitment from their team members. Creating an atmosphere when individuals might talk about past experiences is one way to start in on taking different actions in future situations. For example, ask people to tell you about a time when they felt that they were "stuck" on a problem or ineffective in a situation. The coach can evaluate where the person's thinking or actions didn't work, or better yet, help the person pinpoint these themselves. Ask them to be specific so that you are able to provide pointers about a different way that they could have handled the situation. This often involves helping them break through "old" ways of doing things, and apply some techniques that they may not have tried before. There is true learning that happens when people can recognize their mistakes, and then know how to act in future circumstances. It will help them understand that they may have to be different, think differently, and act differently than they ever have before. All of this will serve to build an individual's self-esteem. The process results in genuine empowerment and in giving people the opportunity to reach their potential. Providing for and coordinating human resources are two important tasks for supervisors. And in our labor-intensive organization, coaching is really the essence of management, because it is getting things done through people.

HOW IS THE SUPERVISOR REWARDED FROM COACHING?

The supervisor does invest a great amount of time in assuming the role of a coach. However, the rewards for doing so are that his or her job is made more productive and perhaps even easier. This is because the technical ability and the skills of the employees who are being supervised are often increased. A team is developed and the supervisor is looked upon as the leader. Overall performance is improved. As a coach you will need to:

- Give advice as necessary
- Hold back advice when experience would be a better teacher
- Recognize when individuals have reached a developmental milestone
- Recognize indirect offers for help
- Provide encouragement
- Provide admiration
- Recognize when performance is not up to par and take appropriate measures
- Support employees even when performance is at a lower than normal level
- Help them recognize areas when they may be "stuck"
- Help them by setting limitations and deadlines and sticking to them

If you follow these points, I believe that you will find that your personal job satisfaction increases.

SHOULD YOU BE A MENTOR?

Here are some things that you should ask yourself if you are considering being a mentor. If you are finding it overwhelming to do all the things in your job as supervisor, it may be better to suggest that some seasoned employees be the mentor until you feel that you can effectively take on this role as well. You can use the following information to help them as well as to help yourself.

Do you like helping less experienced people by . . . ?
   Teaching them a new skill
   Clarifying library and personal professional goals
   Giving them specific information
   Demonstrating the effect that their job responsibilities have

Do you get a feeling of satisfaction in developing others . . . ?
   By recognizing the potential in others
   Providing support and encouragement
   Teaching new sets of skills
   Encouraging others to rise to a challenge
   Giving recognition

Supervisors can transform the workplace. The creative use of talent and experiences can give your library a personal humanized feeling. It gets us beyond the library being the "warehouse" of books, knowledge, etc. It makes the connection that libraries are about people—the professional assisting the patron by helping them identify the information that they need. If you are truly feeling overwhelmed by your new position, you may want to delegate the mentoring process to someone that you feel will perform the job well, and wait until you have the time to devote to the process so that you will do it well.

6 IMPLEMENTING CHANGE AND MANAGING CRISIS

Managing when there is change, even planned change, or in times of trouble is not an easy task. It requires true leadership skills. Of course, the level of management involvement and the seriousness of the conflict will vary from situation to situation. But the axiom holds true—crisis will only be solved by coolheaded action and clear communications that define and deal with the actual problem. Just expect it! Conflict is inevitable! It is an inherent part of humanity. What we must understand is that our job means that we address it, and diffuse it whenever possible. The different problems will require different handling depending upon the situation. It will be different if it is an internal crisis than one that has outside influences. Conflicts can be scary, but many are minor in nature and can be handled relatively simply. Often, it may simply be a matter of the supervisor pointing out to the individuals involved that they need to respect each other's point of view. Managers perform this type of intervention on a daily basis because people are human and they do have trouble interacting. However, from time to time, there may be more mean-spirited conflict. If it is intense, it may even threaten the integrity of the organization. This type of conflict makes it difficult for work to be done and it often can drain the energy not only of the staff members involved, but also of others around them. The tensions that are involved might damage the entire library system if they go unattended. Sometimes minor conflicts may be a symptom of other, deeper problems. It is part of the supervisor's job to recognize this, and be on the alert for them. These types of conflicts may require a solution that is rooted in organizational changes in structure or function. These conflicts may be indicators that it is time for the supervisor to question what is happening in their department and determine if changes are necessary. The supervisor may have to ask her or himself about other issues that have surfaced previously. Are these related to the current situation? And then, they must decide what to do next. It is important that you resist the urge to maintain the status quo. Sure, it is easier than implementing change. But the ability to evolve and adapt is a sign of a much healthier organization and it is the good manager that can make this happen.

BEFORE THE CRISIS OCCURS

Please don't think, "It can't happen to us." Every organization, including libraries, should always be aware that a crisis could occur at any time. It may be the result of an accident, disgruntled employees, terrorism, etc., and it can become a media nightmare. Therefore, the real question is not if a crisis can occur, but rather what can we do when one does happen. There is no single way to solve a crisis; each one has characteristics of its own and it needs to have a unique solution. However, one of the single most effective things to do is to have an emergency crisis plan with designated tasks and designated employees already in place. Practice the plan and test it to see what works and what doesn't. Your crisis team can then discuss alternate ways of handling various situations before they occur. If such a plan is in place, then the library staff will know what steps to take to take care of the immediate solution. Your library will be able to demonstrate concern for individuals within the situation and confidence in your library's ability to assume responsibility and continue its provision of services even where there is a tough situation. Demonstrating concern and the ability to take control is important as the library will have to survive intense scrutiny from outside sources. Once the crisis has occurred, it is imperative that the supervisor asserts him or herself and provides leadership to the staff. The staff will be looking for directions and answers that they can give to the pubic they serve. As a supervisor, you role will be to help the administration develop these solutions, and communicate them to the staff and the public as needed.

Can crisis be avoided or prevented? Sometimes they can be, especially if they are based in a misunderstanding, or in the case of a patron acting disruptively. Sometimes they can be controlled with ground rules as in a demonstration by people around a cause. The following are some tips to remember that might be helpful in dealing with certain episodes. They are useful to keep in mind. As a supervisor, your staff members will call upon you to help them settle disputes. You will be in a position of enforcing library policy while still making the customer feel that he is "right."

1. Be empathetic. It is important not to judge the patron's feelings. They are real—even if they are not based on reality—and the person deserves the right to be listened to.
2. Clarify all messages. Listen "between" the lines to what is really being said. Ask questions and repeat statements

to make sure you understand. Sometimes silence is the best answer—just let the person vent.

3. Try to respect personal space by standing 2 to 3 feet away from the person who is acting out. Don't try to touch them. Using restraining techniques on a person is encroaching on personal space and often has the effect of escalating tension. If you fear that there is going to be a physical attack, ask your co-worker to call for security/police.

4. Be aware of your own body language. Standing eye-to-eye or toe-to-toe sends a message of challenge. Standing off at an angle is less likely to provoke an individual. Be aware of your tone of voice, and movement.

5. Permit verbal venting when possible. This allows the person to release as much energy as possible.

6. Set and enforce reasonable limits even if the person is becoming belligerent, defensive, or disruptive. State the limits in a clear and concise fashion. (Example: Let's move to another area of the library, as there are some people here needing quiet space to study.)

7. How you respond will directly affect the individual's behavior. It is important to remain calm, rational, and professional.

8. Ignore challenge questions. If the patron challenges your position, training, etc., it is better to redirect his or her attention to the issue at hand. Reacting to them on these issues only makes for a power struggle.

CONFLICT ASSESSMENT

We have already indicated that conflict is inevitable; that we should expect it. However, it never is a bad idea to be prepared. You will want to do this as minor issue may escalate into very serious ones if left unattended. Your hard work at team building will be eroded, as concern for self increases when conflict arises.

There are various stages of conflict. The most common type of conflict is caused by the usual day-to-day irritations. Most adults have developed coping strategies that allow us to deal with these and get along with people. Sometimes it is avoidance; we pass things off or ignore them because they really are not important in the overall picture. Obliging behavior is another coping technique. This means that one person may "give in" to another individual. This strategy is used when there is a desire to keep things

On the Job Q & A

Q: The director just informed me of massive changes in my department that will change everyone's job description over the next two years. My staff is afraid that some people will be fired. I honestly don't know if they will or won't. What do I say if they ask me directly?

A: All people are afraid of change, especially when there is no secure feeling that their jobs will remain. First, I would make sure that I have all of the information that I can get from the director. Then, I would make sure that I communicated everything as openly and honestly as I could on a face-to-face basis.

moving. We must accept the fact that when people work together, there are differences in goals, values, and individual needs. If people are willing to separate the personalities from the problem and work for a resolution to the conflict, the following tactics work. As a supervisor, your role is to encourage communication and understanding from both sides. Point out if the reaction to the problem is reasonable or overboard. Identify points of agreement and work with these first before tackling the disagreements. Listening and participation are essential at this level.

However, sometimes there are triggers that will set the conflict off in a stronger direction. Typically, people view these as a "win-lose" situation because people are often tied to the problems. In this second stage, witnesses take sides, verbal victories are recorded, and self-interest issues loom. Coping strategies may not work here because people are the cause of the problem. They resist listening and talking because they have their own view of the issues. In order to manage when this happens, it is important to use specific language. The individuals who are in conflict use words such as "they," or "everyone," and the exaggeration words such as "always" and "never"—these are generalizations, and having people be specific gets at the facts. The first step that the supervisor must take is to be organized and to gather the facts. Again, if you demand accurate, specific facts and not generalizations, you take the step of moving the conflict away from the people and concentrate on the situation. This diffuses bad energy. It may also help to ask various employees to share the responsibility of gathering information. This technique causes the employees to start to think of alternative ways of dealing with the issues as well. Guide employees to find a middle ground, but do not suggest compromise. Compromise implies giving up; instead, it is better to focus on the points that people agree on. Some of these simple steps do work to help solve a situation. However, if you notice that there are comments that focus on either/or, what we call "black or white thinking," you may be in a situation where conflict is going to escalate to a very serious problem.

In the most serious stages, conflicts shift from the attitude of wanting to win toward wanting to hurt. Employees have set their attitudes firmly; they are motivated now by being right, and they want to see wrong punished. Competing employees make people choose sides and factions evolve. A loss of perspective is very likely in these cases. When the conflict has gotten to this stage, one of the most useful tactics is to bring in a neutral party or parties that can help with an intervention. This may lead to mediation, where both sides present their case and the people performing the intervention role facilitates the discussion and helps move the participants to a mutually agreeable and acceptable solution. As a supervisor, you will need to be familiar with negotiation and arbitration as the tools that will bring closure to the situation. Negotiation requires parties to sit across from one another and work through the conflict in the presence of another (often outside) party. Arbitration takes the negotiation process one step further. Each side presents its case; then an outside person makes a decision on what is best for the organization as a whole. The benefit is that there is a clear "winner." The flip side of the coin is that there are also "losers." At the minimum, these individuals must be guided to move on and get their jobs done. Unfortunately in some cases, at this stage, it may mean that some people are let go.

Figure 6.1   Checklist: Organizational Conflict Assessment

Use the following questions to help you assess if there is a conflict situation within your library, and/or to determine how serious a conflict may exist.

Answer Yes or No

1. Are individuals willing to meet and discuss facts?

2. Is there a cooperative spirit?

3. Can individuals discuss issues without involving personalities?

4. Is there a competitive attitude?

5. Is there emphasis on winners and losers?

6. Is it hard to talk about problems without talking about people?

7. Do comments lead you to believe that they were intended to hurt people?

8. Has the organization's good been sacrificed for individual interests?

9. Has there been a loss of middle ground?

10. Is there a choosing of sides?

DEVELOPING THE CRISIS PLAN

Conflict is usually internal, and crisis is most often the result of outside influences. For these situations, advance planning and organization are important. This is because as a supervisor you are also a crisis planner, and crisis planners must anticipate everything that could possibly go wrong! This is true for the "ordinary" types of crisis—fires, hurricanes, earthquakes, etc., and for those that are extreme, such as the terrorist attacks of 9/11. Because there is so much to consider, the development of a crisis plan is best done by a team of people. That will make it more likely that nothing will be overlooked. The first step in developing the plan is to make the most comprehensive list possible of all types of events that could occur. Brainstorming is a good technique to accomplish this. While some ideas may surface that seem extremely unlikely, you should include them anyway. Then, it is a good exercise to rank these with the highest degree of probability for occurring. After that task is complete, you must then adequately address the vulnerabilities of your library in reference to these potential occurrences. Some of the questions that you will want to ask yourself include the following: What is the biggest threat to the health and safety of your employees and visitors? What threatens the library property? What types of interruptions in operations could occur? What could result in the loss of public confidence in your services? Is your library in an area that could be experience blizzards, floods, hurricanes, tornadoes, or other natural disasters? Then, take the time to categorize them as probable or possible. Then think about what steps must be taken first for safety, then to protect services.

Once all of this research is complete, you are in a position to write a crisis plan, and to designate a crisis team. Because the nature of a crisis might knock out your actual facility, it is important to have another designated "emergency control center." This would provide ample working space, communications equipment, and supplies for you to operate and communicate with both staff and others who would be affected by the loss of your services. If you do not have another location to establish such a center, you should talk with the local government officials. Perhaps a school or a fire station or another city facility can spare the space to assist your library if it gets into a crisis mode.

Should you write a plan to address each of the emergency situations that we designated earlier? It is hard to say, but perhaps a solid general plan that is adaptable to a wide variety of emergencies, but leaves the detail of implementation up to the individuals who make up the crisis team, is the best idea. We would suggest that you draft a preliminary outline based on your initial list of possible threats. It is best to proceed in the outline in a logical manner from the lowest threat to the worst-case scenarios. Libraries are great resource sharers, and I would not hesitate to ask a comparable size library to share their information with you and yours with them. Brainstorm with all others supervisors. It is also a good idea to get some input from some outside professionals like a fire marshal, or a police officer as well.

The following are some keys to managing a crisis:

Figure 6.2 Checklist: Steps to Manage Crisis or Emergencies

1. Have a written crisis management plan
   a. Brainstorm possible situations and what actions would be needed to overcome them
   b. Practice the drills
   c. Remember that a crisis is not planned; it is a surprise, and must be dealt with accordingly
   d. The greatest plan is useless if it sits in a file. Share it, practice it, and communicate it to others.

2. Have a crisis team
   a. Select members for their ability to remain objective
   b. Select members who are able to function under scrutiny and pressure (internal and external)
   c. Select members who are flexible
   d. Designate a staff liaison who will remain calm, and remind the staff that the library is in control of the situation; that the crisis will pass, and that there will be a solution to the problem

3. Have a communications plan
   a. Designate a media spokesperson. This person must have expertise on the issue and media experience.
   b. Communicate to all staff members about what is happening. It is important that they have full facts, not rumors, and that they know who will be speaking on behalf of the library.
   c. Have a checklist of questions that need to be answered, with the answers prepared (What happened? Why? What are you doing about it?)
   d. Be current on all library issues, not just the crisis. This is the silver lining—see the crisis as an opportunity to tell your story.
   e. Be prepared to give regular briefings/updates.
   f. It is essential that your library already has established a positive, proactive relationship with the media before the crisis occurs. The quality and quantity of respect you have earned with the media will come in handy.
   g. Develop an early warning system. Be able to detect signs of potential crisis, and drop your regular duties immediately and proceed with the crisis management plan.

4. Be a leader! The Library Director or whoever is designated to be in charge will take command, but leadership is needed on all levels. Begin your assigned tasks and recognize that it is important that you are held accountable for performing them. Remain calm and unemotional and try to exude confidence that the situation is being managed positively.

HANDLING PEOPLE THROUGH CHANGES

As you have seen over and over again, much of the supervisor's job is in handling people. And, one of the most difficult times to handle people is when there is change. People resist change. Introducing new technologies or services can cause some challenging workplace experiences, because people fear change and the unknown. This is especially true if they have not had the opportunity to provide input. It is also because some of the changes that are made as time savers may even cause some job insecurity. Successful change is the result of careful planning, sensitive handling of people, and a thorough approach to the implementation.

Change often demands the acquisition of new skills and the implementation of new practices. It means that the supervisor has to identify the gap between what the present understanding of the task is, and *what* must be learned in order to complete it. It is one thing to know what to do, yet quite another to know *how* to do it. You will also have to identify the hard-core resisters, those who are most actively against the change, and work with them first, if at all possible. Failure to do so may open the window so that they can influence others and then you will have a bigger problem on your hands.

One of the most successful ways that you can reduce resistance to change is by providing your employees with as much notice as possible, and by communicating to them why the change is necessary. Let them see your own commitment to the change; listen to their concerns; and demonstrate how this change is going to be better for the library. Here are some real-life examples. We had a situation when our city announced that payday would move from Thursdays to Fridays. It does not seem like something as small as this would be a big problem, but people began to complain just because something was different. When they were presented with the information that this process in that particular year would move one pay date into another budget year (creative finance on the city's part!) and thus save the city an enormous amount of money, they began to understand. Electronic deposit also was a cost-saving method that the city implemented. People resisted it but when it was understood that it would help prevent job freezes or layoffs, the move then made sense to them. A more complicated change occurred when our automated circulation system moved from a "dumb" terminal to a PC-based environment. Computerphobia, among our circulation staff especially,

On the Job Q & A

Q: Has something like this ever happened to you?

A: I can remember waking up one Saturday morning to newspaper headlines that there would be massive layoffs throughout the city because of a budget shortfall. Although I was not scheduled to be at work, I hurried out the door, stopped for donuts and coffee, and called an emergency meeting of my staff members. I told them all that I knew at that point and assured them that I would keep them informed as best as I could when I received information from the city manager, not the newspaper! I heard later on that they appreciated my efforts and honesty.

was rampant at first. But clear communication about why the process was necessary and adequate training opportunities for all overcame the strong-willed resistance from some of the long-time staff.

What are some of the common reasons why change is necessary in libraries? First, new technologies are constantly being developed, and as we take advantage of their capabilities, we are able to use them to make our work more efficient and, at times, easier. Sometimes change is necessary because we have limited resources, or reduced resources and we have to find ways of providing the same services or different services anyway. We may look to find other ways to do things, or to eliminate steps that might be as critical. We will want to adapt the best procedures and have the best structures in place. Change happens because the administration has decided that it is the right thing to do for the future. And, in general, change is good for us! It is desirable and it is achievable. It provides a growth opportunity, and we learn from it! Change is one of the things that makes jobs exciting and eliminates boredom.

There are four critical steps that people go through with the change process and supervisors should be aware they happen. The first step is denial. Because change is difficult, people often will not believe that it is going to happen. They refuse to acknowledge it and may even ignore the planning or early stages of implementation. The second phase is resistance. Because of the fears associated with change, people will often do everything that they can think of in order to prevent the change from happening. They may even believe that the change is not necessary and that it won't work. The third phase is exploration. This is achieved by the supervisor's intervention and providing information to the employee about how the changes will impact their work. The supervisor should also explain that not taking new actions could have more serious repercussions than going along with the plan. The change is demonstrated and the employee is able to see that it is not as "bad" as they thought. The final phase is acceptance, when the employee comes to realize that this is the way things will be happening in their workplace, and they must do what they are told if they are going to keep their job. As the supervisor, you must be the role model and have a positive attitude about the change, and enforce the new procedures.

STYLES OF MANAGING PEOPLE

People are different, and so supervisors and their styles differ. In the management of all fields, there are recognized "styles." However, in my experience, very few people are one style or another all of the time. They usually have tendencies toward one style, but may adopt characteristics of a different one in order to meet the demands of a particular situation. You will have to decide which style is best for you. You need to consider your own personality and the personalities that you supervise in your particular library. Along with this, you will want to consider the various nuisances that a situation brings. An excellent book and a great resource on the topic is *Type Talk at Work* by Otto Kroeger and Janet Thuesen.

SAMPLE STYLES

Below are some of the recognized management styles that are commonly found.

Command/directive	Staff has little or no input; supervisor gives orders, employees follow them.
Supportive	May be compassionate and understanding, but some supervisors may do a great deal of hand-holding. There is a danger of micromanaging with this style so the supervisor should be careful.
Laissez-faire	The supervisor delegates, maybe even a little too much. It can provide a great growth opportunity for employees. It is important to remember to follow up on goals and objectives.
Socratic	The supervisor hears ideas, but does not discuss them with the employees. Rather, he or she asks them to think their idea through and come to some conclusion of what should be done.

Participative   Employees are asked by the supervisor to share responsibility in the workplace by being forthcoming with their ideas. The best methods for the whole are the ones that are implemented. The more that people feel comfortable that they can contribute and make a difference, the more positive they will feel about work.

All of the above are descriptions of management styles that have been used successfully by managers. Each supervisor will have to determine which elements of each of the styles that fit their personality and their workplace best. Coaching, as described in another chapter, can help you avoid that "one size fits all" type of management style. It will help you see that you may need to deal with employees on an individual basis in order to be successful with them. At the same time, you must remember that you must treat all employees fairly. Each person will also have to remember that there are also mistakes that undermine productivity. These include a supervisor who "doesn't practice what he or she preaches"; one who promises to share decision–making, but doesn't; and domination or "dictatorship" in the workplace, which is often viewed as disrespect for employees' ideas and values. You must always remember that good management does not mean lowering your performance standards so that people can achieve them. Rather, it means that you help the individuals develop the skills necessary to achieve, and offer them the opportunities to do so.

CONFLICT MANAGEMENT

Conflict management is necessary in any workplace that employs more than one person! It is the nature of humans to disagree. That is not always a bad thing. Conflicting ideas often result in high-quality outcomes because people have considered alternatives and are forced to reach consensus on the best idea for the particular situation.

At other times, there are conflicts that arise for unnecessary reasons, and they do get in the way of work and productivity. Supervisors have the responsibility to help staff members cope with their problems whenever necessary, as the conflicts may interfere with the work that is to be done.

Some common sources of conflict include those caused by individuals who put their own self-interests and agenda before the good of the whole; staff members who do not "see the big picture" because they are so absorbed in their own job function; rules or policies that haven't been fully developed; staff members who are not mutually respectful and open to all ideas; and staff members who have values or beliefs that are contrary to the library's mission and goals.

As a supervisor, you have the challenge of finding ways of taking these potential volatile situations and finding a way of having staff work together. The *cause* of the conflict must be addressed or the conflict will not go away. As we discussed earlier in our chapter on team building, individuals may resent being put on a particular work team for a variety of reasons. But, if you are a strong coach, doing exactly this can help you meet the library's goals. Individuals are forced (because they must if they are going to keep their job—a great motivator!) to develop shared views; they are forced to consider processes from different perspectives. As the supervisor, your job is to provide these individuals with the skills that can help them be successful at this. After all, you do want success for the library.

Bargaining is one of the techniques that we can recommend. You teach people how to "deal." That is, you help them evaluate what is absolutely essential to them, learn what it is that their "opponents" want, and then help them realize how they are willing to compromise. This usually will result in a resolution that is comfortable to all. If you confront problems by putting every thing out on the table, solutions become clearer, and a positive outlook by all is much more likely to occur.

Another technique is simply common-sense problem-solving. In this method, you get the various representatives of the different sides of the issue to define the problem as they see it based on facts. Once this information is clear, then collaboratively, the people work on alternative solutions that are best for all.

Another issue to keep in mind is the need for research. This is especially important if you have the feeling that opinions, rather than facts, are on the table. Take the time and gather the data or have employees work on it. Researching for information is a core function of the library and it is important that we put our skills to work for us. Research can also be accomplished through surveys, focus groups, or reading. Finally, there is the old standby of voting. While it seems that this would be the democratic thing to do, this process actually has its disadvantages. Even when people have their vote, there are still "winners" and "losers," and the losers are less likely to embrace the decision than they would if they had been led to reach a compromise or consensus for the situation.

The important thing is to make sure that the fundamentals of problem-solving are in place and that they then are interpreted correctly. That is the supervisor's job. If you have established an atmosphere of trust within your workplace, the opportunity to foster creative solutions is there. As a supervisor, you can do this by being consistent in meeting commitments; by providing reliable information/communications on a regular basis; by demonstrating your skills; and by showing sincere interest in the ability, views, and the involvement of others. Although conflicts in the workplace are the natural consequences of human interactions, you can see that they are not all bad. There are lessons to be learned by all of us about attitudes, adjustment, and on-the-job relationships. In fact, conflict should be seen as an opportunity for creative problem-solving and for employee development. The supervisor must make sure that there is consistent respect for others point of view. That is when conflict will be turned into collaboration.

Sometimes conflict is created by poor planning. Obstacles that impede progress and cause conflict include not having the right "players" on the team; not having a complementary mix of personalities; lack of adequate support and resources to perform a job; and lack of effective leadership. If conflict is personality-related, it is important to get people to talk with one another openly and let each other know how their behavior is affecting them. The longer that this is not confronted, the more uncomfortable people are going to be. These matters need to be confronted and then steps taken to meet the necessary resolution.

Everyone needs to recognize that change is what happens in life; it is a surety. As individuals, we can create and embrace change, or we can fear and fight it. However, change *will* come in either case.

Solving problems means that you first have to take the steps to define exactly what the problem is, and what the probable causes for it are. Then possible solutions must be developed along with the necessary actions to implement them. And, interestingly enough, sometimes crisis is what will bring the people in an organization together with a common cause. Then they see that the little everyday issues are not that important.

> **Figure 6.3 Checklist: Ground Rules for Collaboration at Work**
>
> - Use professional courtesy at all times
>
> - Establish common ground with others
>
> - Watch your language—is it work-appropriate?
>
> - Ask for help when you need it
>
> - Make small talk work for you
>
> - Use appropriate humor
>
> - Avoid hostility
>
> - Confront interpersonal issues privately
>
> - Know where boundaries start and end

TALKING TO THE MEDIA IN TIMES OF CRISIS

As part of an overall library system, as a supervisor you may or may not have a role to play with the media in the time of crisis. Your library may have a spokesperson who has this specific charge. However, it is good to have some idea of the accepted plan and process in case you are the one that the media reaches. Remember, in times of crisis, you must facilitate the factual flow of information without letting any negative, emotionally charged issues take over. Here are some basic rules to follow in these situations.

- Be prepared! Keep a list of the most important facts on a small card near your phone. This will help your message as being perceived as credible because you do not hesitate about giving answers. If you have a situation in which you truly do not have the answer, tell the reporter that you will find out and get back to them with it. Then do.
- If you have fostered good relationships during routine times, the press will most likely not view you as part of the problem.

- Anticipate some of the questions that you might receive about some possible problems (censorship, filtering, etc.). Prepare answers, and rehearse them in quiet times. This will make you better prepared when the inevitable happens.
- Do not be afraid to admit an error or problem. Balance the negative with the appropriate show of concern, or plans to rectify the problem. Do not be afraid to admit that you do not have an answer to a given question. No one can expect you to know everything. Take the time to find out, and then let them know the answer. This is much more preferable than giving out incorrect information.
- Don't become angry and upset at the questioning. Stay calm and keep the situation in perspective.
- Take the initiative to make the points that you want to make during an interview. If this is your only chance to get your information out to the public, then you must say it even if it does not specifically relate to the question asked. Take advantage of the opportunity.
- Don't ever lie. If you want to maintain credibility, it is much better to say that you choose not to answer the question, or that you will answer it at another time, or whatever is true.
- Be available. Never have "no comment." If you feel that someone else should answer (Board President or attorney), say that instead!

In times of crisis, how you handle a situation is just as important as the final outcome. If you are prepared, and composed, you will have a much better chance of handling the situation effectively. After the crisis has passed, remember that you still have the challenge of renewing proactive media contacts. As you communicate, your messages should reflect that the library is taking responsibility for the resolution of the crisis at hand, and if it is appropriate, reinforce the library's record and commitment to making things right. If the result is a change in plan, services, etc., those affected should be updated as frequently and as often as the situation changes.

It is important that those in charge, the supervisors, remain visible through the crisis and not hide behind the scenes. This is true even if there is an official spokesperson. The spokesperson can also assist you with your comments, or tell you when deference to a spokesperson in a given situation is more appropriate. And, probably the most important thing to remember is the rea-

---

On the Job Q & A

Q: What can I do to encourage my staff should a situation like this occur?

A: I would encourage people to continue to do the best that they can in their current jobs. The quality of their work could be a factor in being considered for other work in the library in the event that their current jobs get eliminated. I would also plan as much training as possible to encourage them to develop their skills. Knowing that you will be forthcoming and honest with information will help build their trust in you.

son why you are working at the library in the first place. Continue to provide excellent library service!

Every press statement should be preceded by a thorough review of the library's position and policies that relate to the particular situation. This reiteration makes it clear to the outside world that you have carefully thought out steps to deal with the crisis. In terms of policy, it means that a Board of Directors has created a "rule" for the benefit of the whole. Any hesitancy in formulating responses to questions may be viewed as a sign of confusion, deception, unconcern, or incompetence. Management must stay firm and clear and project the truth to its stakeholders at all times. The challenge is to be able to define the true problem, set short-term objectives, and rapidly deploy methods that will be a solution.

Managerial performance is a combination of knowledge and skills and the application of these skills in actual circumstances. It is important that you exhibit professional behavior at all times. All work, in libraries and in the world, has circumstances that create problems. Being able to navigate them successfully will be the standard upon which you will be measured as a supervisor. Figure 6.4 gives helpful hints on how to deal with people.

Figure 6.4   Checklist: Coping Skills in Dealing with Difficult People

- Stop wishing "they" will change; they won't. Learn how to deal with them.

- Don't take it personally. If a person is difficult, it is their problem. If you take it personally it becomes your problem. Focus on the task at hand instead.

- Do try to understand why they are acting in a particular way.

- Find a middle ground. Manage your feelings, and base your confrontations on facts not emotions.

- Keep a sense of humor.

- Take a deep breath. The pause will help you think more clearly.

And finally, one of the best pieces of advice that I was even given, was to know myself. If you are going to be successful as a people manager, it is important that you first develop a strong sense of your own self-worth. You need to value your profession, and respect and honor the people that you work with. Then, you will be able to work with change and crisis and to continue to connect people to ideas, which is the essence of true librarianship.

7 USING PERFORMANCE APPRAISALS EFFECTIVELY

Taking over as a supervisor demands immediate evidence of your ability to take charge and to recognize what your employees are capable of achieving. The people that you are now supervising may feel a little cautious or even a little doubting of your ability to be able to do this. However, through a combination of talking with them, and with your own observations you should be able to do this. If you are going to become a successful manager, you will need to develop your style and your skills. Most likely the staff will be in place and you will need to be flexible and adapt your style to encourage them to perform. Your future as a manager depends on your ability to have productive employees. The performance of employees is what will determine the success of the library.

WHY DO WE EVALUATE EMPLOYEES?

Probably one of the tasks that most supervisors find the most difficult is completing employee performance ratings or evaluations. This is probably because it is difficult to call attention to areas of a person's work that may need improvement without hurting his or her feelings. And yet, it is one of the most essential tasks that a supervisor can perform to be of service to the library. It is our responsibility to help people develop to do the jobs that we need done. Probably one of the misconceptions that many people have is that this is a task that should be done once a year. In truth, evaluating performance needs to be done continuously. The first one that you do for an employee sets up a baseline so that both you and the employee can measure progress. My advice on the best way to do it is to focus on the strengths that employees are exhibiting. One of your tasks will be to communicate to them that the mission of the library is bigger than any one person's ability to carry out. They will need to understand that each person's work is important to achieve it. This in itself makes people feel that they can make a difference with the job that they do.

On the Job Q & A

Q: How can I get staff to follow directions?

A: Role-playing can be an invaluable tool in management. Pick fictitious yet realistic situations. Ask two or more people to act out the situation. Make it a randomly selected one, and give them no preparation time. Results can be very interesting. (Examples of situations: interviewing three candidates for a position; dealing with a difficult patron.)

WHEN DO WE DO EVALUATIONS?

The effective supervisor should be evaluating at all stages of work. This begins with setting goals—asking the question if these are appropriate goals for this position. It continues with observing implementation steps that lead to achieving the goals. And finally, there always should be a retrospective look back once tasks have been completed. Looking at goals and objectives perhaps may be the single most important step of the process because it helps employees understand the benefit that their work will have on the library. If you have determined that there is some deficiency, then there is a need to follow up or use a corrective process if necessary. Supervisors always have to be evaluating the people who work for them, but also the events for which they are responsible, materials, facilities, and other related issues. This does not mean that the supervisor is a watchdog who instills fear, or tries to control or approve everything that happens. Rather, evaluation is an interactive process that provides encouragement and reinforcement. This process can create an exciting and involved workplace.

THE PERFORMANCE APPRAISAL IS A SUPERVISORY TOOL

Performance evaluations are an essential and effective means of addressing a variety of employment-related matters. While this is a formal process that provides a framework for discussing the overall work of the employee, the information that is gathered on a daily basis can be addressed in an informal manner. Evaluations are important because they let employees know how they are doing. They are also helpful so that together you can set reasonable performance goals for the future. The process provides a way for the supervisor to maximize the employee's potential, create a teamwork atmosphere, and to improve the overall operation. The dedicated employee receives a minimum of pats on the back and the less than dedicated employee is provided counsel to improve.

In an effort to be sensitive to employees' feelings, supervisors are sometimes unwilling to confront employees with performance problems. The best rule is to be honest and to use job-specific questions in order to achieve the best results. Consistency is also important in demonstrating that you are being fair to all.

The best way to convey the results of a performance evaluation is through private, face-to-face meetings with each employee. Sharing feedback is essential to keeping open communications and to achieve improved performance. The employee also has the opportunity to talk with you. He or she may be frustrated by a task or a process. He or she may not understand the necessity of the task they have been asked to do or how it relates to other tasks within the library. Perhaps some employees have even found a better way to achieve the same result but they are a little reserved about coming forward with it in front of other employees. They may even been having some personality clashes with their co-workers and may not know how to deal with them. The opportunity to meet with you privately gives employees some sense of security to discuss these issues. Your discussion will strengthen your relationship and make the overall process of evaluation much more meaningful.

Figure 7.1 provides a tool that can be used to set a baseline of employee performance. It documents that the job expectations were clearly communicated to the individuals and alerts the supervisor to follow up on achievement. It is less formal than the annual appraisal and can be used after any length of time—i.e., after a particular project, every three months, etc.

Figure 7.1   Sample: Performance Feedback Tool

This is a good process to follow on an interim basis to keep track of employee progress.
   Take the time to sit down with each employee and use the feedback to help them improve on their job.

Employee:

Position:

Pay Grade:

Supervisor:

Start Date:

End Date:

Objectives: List a minimum of three objectives and indicate status.

Customer Service Delivery:

Project Status:

Quality of performance:

Teamwork:

Adherence to policies:

Work Ethic:

Plan for future achievement:

Employee comments:

On the Job Q & A

Q: What are some questions to ask about program evaluation?

A: Ask yourself questions about interrelationships, especially in cross-functional interrelationships. Try to imagine every bottleneck that can occur, and think of an alternative approach. Ask regularly how things are going.

There are many different versions of performance appraisal and evaluation forms. Some are required by particular government agencies or by labor unions. The best practice is for the supervisor to inquire about the forms and/or system that may be in place at your particular library. If you find that the appraisal form is cumbersome or not helpful, you can research and recommend the use of another type of form. In the event that you are required to complete a form that you feel is less than helpful, I would also recommend devising your own process. You can then use the information that you have recorded as talking points with your employees, and the formal process for the legal records. This is not to say that I recommend ignoring the importance of following procedures. Do both! It is always more useful to gather the data that you feel will be most helpful in improving the work productivity of your staff but it is also important to meet system requirements. The little extra time that it may take will be well worth the effort.

Figure 7.2   Sample: Performance Appraisal Form

These are some sample categories that often appear on performance appraisal forms that can be used annually to rate employee performance. These are intended to be suggestions that can be used in addition to forms that your organization my already have. Their contents can also be adapted into new forms for your library that evaluate exactly what you need to know to help your employees improve.

Employee Name:_____ Job Title_____Date _____

Supervisor: _____

Instructions: Select the description that best describes the employee performance.

Job Elements	Good		Needs Improvement		
Knowledge of Work	Well informed	Thorough	Adequate	Needs assistance	Inadequate
Quantity of Work	Very productive	Good volume	Average	Below Average	Slow worker
Quality of Work	Exceptionally Accurate	Few errors	Acceptable	Many errors	Unacceptable

Ability to Learn

New Duties	Quick to learn Adaptable	Retains instruction	Average	Needs great deal of help	Slow learner
Initiative	Resourceful Creative	Timely, handles work	Occasional	Rarely	Needs
Cooperation	Goes beyond	Gets along	Acceptable	Reluctant	Poor
Judgment	Outstanding Logic	Usually Good	Fairly	Illogical	Unreliable

Other:

Comments:

Suggestions for improvements:

Overall	Excellent	Good	Satisfactory	Fair	Unsatisfactory

Signature Of Employee: _____

Signature of Supervisor: _____

Figure 7.3   Sample: Employee Performance Evaluation

Employee Name _____

Job Title _____

Period Covered: Date:

Immediate Supervisor:

Instructions: This form is designed to allow the supervisor to evaluate the employee's performance. Each area should be discussed with the employee with suggestions for improvement.

Instructions: This form is designed to allow the supervisor to evaluate the employee's performance. Each area should be discussed with the employee with suggestions for improvement.
*Rankings: 5 Excellent; 4 Very Good; 3 Satisfactory; 2 Conditional ; 1 Warning(Not acceptable
performance) Please circle.*

1. Position Knowledge
*This is the degree to which the employee understands the function of the position and uses the
resources necessary to gain the knowledge to perform it.*

Rating   5   4   3   2   1

Comments: _____

2. Work Quality
This category includes accuracy, neatness, completion of assignments, and attention to detail.

Rating   5   4   3   2   1

Comments: _____

3. Productivity
*This is the volume of work that is completed and the effective use of resources so that the em-
ployee makes the best use of his/her time.*

Rating   5   4   3   2   1

Comments: _____

Figure 7.3   Sample: Employee Performance Evaluation (*Continued*)

4. Teamwork

This indicates how well the employee is able to work with others and how they respect others' ideas.

Rating   5   4   3   2   1

Comments: _____

5. Dependability

This is the degree to which the employee can be relied upon to follow instructions, complete assigned tasks, and to attend meetings.

Rating   5   4   3   2   1

Comments: _____

6. Judgment

This measures the degree with which the employee uses sound reasoning to make decisions, making sure that he/she has the necessary data to do so.

Rating   5   4   3   2   1

Comments: _____

7. Initiative

This is the employee's willingness to accept responsibility and to work independently. They are eager to learn new methods to accomplish work.

Rating   5   4   3   2   1

Comments: _____

8. Adaptability

This reflects the employee's ability to work under changed or new situations or working conditions.

Rating   5   4   3   2   1

Comments: _____

Figure 7.3   Sample: Employee Performance Evaluation (*Continued*)

---

9. Work Planning
This indicates the employee's ability to organize work and accomplish assignments.

Rating   5   4   3   2   1

Comments: _____

---

10. Overall Evaluation
Depending upon your organization's policy, these may also need to be signed by the Library Director or the Human Resources Manager.

As an employee, you too will receive evaluations. I have always felt that it is a good idea to use a standard form and to evaluate *yourself* as honestly as you can. This technique will help you be prepared to discuss the various areas that may need improving with your supervisor. It will also help you develop some goals to work on for the following year. It is interesting that many employees will rate themselves much more strictly than their supervisor. So, it usually is a pleasant surprise when the actual appraisal session happens.

Figure 7.4   Sample: Supervisor's Performance Appraisal

Supervisor: _____Period Covered:_____Date of Appraisal: _____

Director:_____

Part I: Objectives

	Met	Exceeded	Not Yet Met

1.

2.

3. *Please note: The number will vary by position and in different library systems.*

Part II. *Assign Rating Number to each. Excellent=5, Outstanding=4, Good=3, Fair 2, Not acceptable =1*

Planning: Sets realistic goals; anticipates and prepares for future; establishes priorities; designs and evaluates procedures to meet objectives. Rating:

Organizing: Allocates resources; assigns responsibilities; delegates authority; coordinates programs. Rating:

Directing: Establishes procedures; motivates and trains staff; makes operating decisions.

Rating:

Controlling: Measures and evaluates results against plans; controls workloads; keeps deadlines. Rating:

Productivity: Produces expected amount of work. **Rating:**

Quality: Correctness, completeness, accuracy, and efficiency with which work is done.

Rating:

Use of Time: Manages available time wisely; ability to complete work within established schedule.

Rating:

Interpersonal Relations: This is the ability to establish a cordial, harmonious work climate and works well with others. **Rating:**

Figure 7.4   Sample: Supervisor's Performance Appraisal (*Continued*)

Leadership: Sets high standards, provides managerial model, motivates. **Rating:**

Initiative: Self-motivated, self reliant, resourceful, willing to seek new solutions to carry out responsibilities. **Rating:**

Communication: Expresses thought and ideas orally and in writing and listens well. **Rating:**

Judgment: Is able to make sound decisions based on mature reasoning and acceptance of consequences. Analyzes problems and develops logical solutions. **Rating:**

Flexibility: Adjusts effectively to a variety of changing situations; adaptable. **Rating:**

Quality and Frequency of Interactions with Other Employees:

Overall Rating:

Comments from Director:

Comments of employee:

Signature of employee:_____ Date: _____

Signature of Director: _____ Date: _____

On the Job Q & A

Q: How do I handle a troublemaker?

A: First you must decide why you have classified the employee as a troublemaker. Is it because he or she has done something that is not constructive or disruptive to the library? Or is it because he or she has made some suggestions that are different than those presented in a meeting?

In the first case, I believe that a one-to-one discussion will help you get to the root of the problem. Some people need attention, and maybe that is all this employee was seeking. In the second case, I would argue that the person is not necessarily a troublemaker. Rather, he or she is expressing different thoughts as we should be encouraging our staff to do. This is the beauty of a democratic society—the right to express different opinions. While management may decide that these different ideas are not the most effective for a particular situation, it is good management practice to listen and to help the individual learn why another approach may be better. And, surprise! Many times there will be great ideas that you haven't thought of!

AVOIDING COMMON ERRORS IN THE APPRAISAL PROCESS

A key to improved employee evaluations and appraisals is the development of the rating abilities of the supervisor. You should take advantage of any workshops or seminars that are available for this reason. As a supervisor, you will soon learn that you are frequently making judgments about employees on an informal basis. You recognize their cooperation or lack of it. You look at quantity and the quality of their work. You note if they are dependable and punctual. While these are informal evaluating techniques, they are the basis of learning the larger skill of employee evaluation.

Perhaps one of the most important things that every supervisor needs to learn is the importance of documentation. Good documentation will enable a third party, who may be asked to review an employee's record, to come to the same appraisal conclusions as you have. You will want to keep a careful record of concrete successes; of skills learned; and of problems that the employee has been able to solve. You will also want to note a tendency to careless mistakes; any knowledge or skill gaps that you have observed; any problems that have arisen. Always date and time these observations, especially when they indicate a deficiency. It is human nature that employees will try to defend themselves and deny that an incident happened. It is also important that you don't document rumors. You should never quote other people's comments or opinions. You are the supervisor; it is your observation that is important for the employee. You document only facts. You will also want to avoid any personal comments about employees. It is always better to keep the appraisal focused on job performance and ability to complete tasks rather than on the employee as a person.

On the Job Q & A

Q: During a performance appraisal, one of my staff members started crying and divulging very personal information. How do I act compassionately but professionally?

A: It is important that you remain calm and let the person cry for a while. Crying itself releases tension. This also gives you some time to think through what you will say to the person. You will need to determine if the information is related to the person's ability to perform his or her job. If it is, and there is something further that you can do to provide support, tell him or her what it is and follow through. It may require a change in work schedule to make things work out at home. If the problems are truly personal and not related to work, it is always good practice to refer the person to the Employee Assistance Program, if your library has one. Assure the person that meeting with this provider is totally confidential. If you have a level of comfort with the person talking to you, he or she may indeed just need a sympathetic ear. Listen for the person to tell you that it helped to talk to you—you may not have to say anything if he or she just need to vent. Let the person know that your door is open if he or she needs to talk again. In any case, I would be very careful about giving advice. It is always appropriate to recommend speaking with someone at the person's church/synagogue, as clergy members are trained to counsel.

Figure 7.5 Checklist: Common Appraisal Process Errors

Try to avoid these and your experience and that of your employees will be so much better.

- The standards that are set are poor, or communicated poorly to the employee

- Not enough time is set aside for the observation and appraisal process

- Watch if you spend more time talking to rather than listening to an employee

- There has been a lack of adequate training

- Lack of documentation, or invalid documentation

- Rating everyone the same because you are afraid of hurting feelings

- Your tone of voice and demeanor is threatening

- You haven't set aside enough time for this evaluation interview

- Being too lenient or too strict. Extremes can create unrealistic expectations.

Following the tips listed in Figure 7.6 will help you in developing your evaluation skills.

Figure 7.6   Checklist: Tips for How to Evaluate Successfully

- Employee must accept the standards by which he/she will be measured

- Keep records, positive and negative of employee performance and behavior

- Review any pertinent written information before making your assessment

- Don't discuss generalities; refer to specific situations

- Point out implementations of actions and how they impact the department's performance

- Don't avoid issues because you believe your discussion will then become unpleasant. This will allow a bad situation to get worse.

On the Job Q & A

Q: How can I avoid performance appraisal mistakes?

A: Keep good records. Document good as well as poor performance, and what was done about it. Don't assess an employee as "outstanding" because of only one impressive trait or accomplishment. Consider everything. Likewise, do not judge an employee on one poor incident and forget about all past incidents in which the employee did well. Prepare by reviewing documentation. Don't give the employee the impression that you are judging him or her by pointing out mistakes or faults. Stick to an assessment based on established goals and how well they were met.

ACCOMMODATION

If an employee is not doing well in a particular job, it may be that he or she is in one for which they are not suited. If you feel that the employee is a valuable one, rather than terminating them, you may want to transfer them into a job that is more in keeping with their capabilities. If you have invested time and money into training the person, this is a good route to take if you have the capability of doing so. Your role as a supervisor is to get the employee to agree that there is a need for a change in their work. In many cases, they are already aware that another set of tasks might be better for them. So be honest, and listen to their input as well as communicating your observations. Once the decision to make a change has been implemented, follow through with support for the individual.

Check on the employee and see how they are now working. With this process as well, it is important that you set a timetable for their adaptation. They need to know that you do have expectations that must be met. Recognize their efforts at becoming a valuable employee and follow up with them regularly.

On the Job Q & A

Q: How do I tactfully but forcefully confront "areas that need improvement" during the performance appraisal?

A: First of all, focus on the problem. Do not bring emotions into the discussion. Stick to the facts. Remain objective. Don't dictate a solution to the employee. Rather, have him or her suggest ways to improve. You can agree with this, conveying that you value this employee and that you think he or she can make the change.

If you use simple common sense and humanity and apply these characteristics consistently, you will help people improve their competency. Nothing will affect an employee's desire to do better than the recognition of the supervisor's sensitivity and concern about them.

Performance appraisals are useful tools for several different management functions. They can serve as a basis of decisions relating to promotion or termination. It is the way that outstanding workers are justly compensated and it can help weed out poor performers. The systematic written assessment of a worker by different people over time helps back up these decisions. If the time is spent to conduct these appraisals properly, they facilitate understanding between supervisors and employees. The process is intended to help employees establish personal goals that will enable them to develop and thus be able to further the goals of the library. While the process is not perfect, if standards are used and employees understand how and why they are so rated, the library can only benefit. The Director and top leaders of the organization should make it clearly understood to all employees that it expects everyone to take this task seriously.

WHAT USES ARE MADE OF EVALUATIONS

Employee evaluation requires one person to make an official judgment about another person. Few supervisors like this role, and few employees like to be rated. But, if you are still in doubt as to why these appraisals should be done, review the following.
Evaluations:

1. Keep employees informed of what is expected and how well they are performing
2. Recognize and reward good work
3. Help a supervisor recognize a deficiency and remedy it
4. Identify further training needs
5. Provide a continuing record of employee's performance history
6. Serve as a guide for promotions, transfers, etc.
7. Help determine if and how much of a pay raise should be granted to an employee (merit systems)
8. Checks on the reasonableness of established performance standards

9. Checks on the accuracy of job descriptions and classifications
10. Check on the effectiveness of recruitment, orientation, and training processes

3 HIRING AND RETAINING A DIVERSE WORKFORCE

There are different models of staffing patterns in different libraries. These models may vary depending upon the type of library which is dependent upon its user needs and its location. Some libraries rely on part-time staff or on call workers, while others have unionized professional and support staff. Some even use temporary employees or contractors. The information that is included within this chapter is an example of what might be appropriate in a library. You may use it as a guide with which to measure your local policies. There is no one "perfect" way to manage personnel. Communities differ in their expectations of their employees. Workweeks may vary in length, as will benefits. Please remember that local policies and procedures take precedence. If you are a public library, your policies should be consistent with the city's. If you are an academic library, the policy should be consistent with policy on other parts of the campus.

ELEMENTS OF A PERSONNEL POLICY

The following is a list of items that are important to consider when developing a personnel policy.

Affirmative action | This is a positive action that is taken to ensure equal employment opportunity for all.

Benefits | This may include unemployment insurance, retirement/pension plans, medical insurance, life insurance, purchasing books at discount rates, membership in a credit union or professional organization.

Job descriptions | A job description is a statement of expected performance. It should include: job title; kind and extent of skills, knowledge, and abilities required; relation to service to the public; major performance responsibilities; chain of supervision.

Employees need job descriptions to differentiate between similar jobs and to provide clarity and understanding between employee and supervisor in understanding exactly what is expected.

Hours

Every employee should know what their workweek will be and their schedule. There should be a description of the number of hours an employee is expected to work, and the length and frequency of rest breaks. Some libraries allow for "flextime" which would allow the employee to begin and end work at other than regular hours. Usually this is done for the benefit of both the employer and the employee. Because libraries are public service organizations, all employees should understand that they will be required to work Saturdays, Sundays, and evenings depending upon the particular situation at your library. A pay or time differential should be established for these hours.

Overtime

Many libraries do not have this benefit, but rather adapt schedules through flextime to accommodate extra hours. Overtime traditionally is defined as any time over the regularly assigned hours for additional pay.

Compensatory time

This is time acquired by an employee working more than regular hours without overtime pay with the approval of the director.

The time is then taken at a time that is approved by the director.

Emergency closings

The decision to close the library temporarily is usually made by the Director and/or the Board President. Employees are paid for this closing. If the library is open during snowstorms or other "emergency" situations, then employees who do not come to work must be charged sick, personal, or vacation time.

Holidays

The library follows a schedule of holidays that usually conforms with the town or academic community. Holidays that are authorized by law are paid days off. If a holiday falls on a weekend, another day should be designated.

Vacations

A paid vacation is earned by workers at a rate that is determined by local custom, or contract. The time off must be subject to approval by the supervisor or the Director so that the library can continue to operate effectively. Usually, employees are required to take vacation during the year in which it was earned and not carried over to the next year. There may be a waiting period before an employee make take time off. Part-time workers may get paid vacation depending upon the local custom.

Sick leave

Sick leave means the absence of any employee because of illness, accident, medical/dental appointments, or attendance upon a sick member of the immediate family. The number of days per year is determined by local custom/contract; 15 is an example. Some systems allow employees to accumulate a certain number of days (90, 120); in some cases, employees who do not use their sick time are compensated for it monetarily. The administration may require proof of illness, especially for more than three

	consecutive days. Abuse of sick leave may be the cause of disciplinary action.
Other leave	Employees must be given leave when subpoenaed for jury duty, military duty, or emergency civilian duty. Family leave is granted under federal law for pregnancy, paternity, and other medical conditions of family members. Bereavement absence for deaths within the immediate family is another type of paid leave. Most organizations provide between three and five paid days. Some communities allow personal leave without pay in special cases.
Professional meetings	Most libraries encourage participation in educational and professional activities that are work-related. Time with pay, the registration fees, travel expenses may be included when financially possible. These meetings keep staff current in new developments in the field and attendance at them should be approved by the Director.
Continuing education	Improvement of library services to users is the primary purpose of continuing education for employees. This may involve updating or refreshing a person's education, diversifying with new skills especially in light of changing technologies and processes.
Probationary Period	In many circumstances, new employees are probationary. This is a trial period of adjustment in which the supervisor can judge employees' ability.
Performance appraisal	Employees must have their job expectations given to them at the start of their employment, and they should be evaluated on a regular timetable.

Employee evaluations should always be in writing, and should be included in the personnel file along with any comments that the employee makes about the appraisal. Signatures of the employee, the supervisor, and the Director are usually included as well. The purpose of the appraisal is to account for productivity; to plan and set future goals; to develop personnel for potential position changes; to set up conditions to achieve motivation; to justify pay increases; and to identify hidden potential within employees. This process helps employees make progress in their work and learn where they stand in the minds of their supervisors. Performance evaluations are a factor in determining salary increases, promotions, reclassifications, and dismissals.

Grievances

As long as people work together, there will always be a certain amount of real and/or imagined grievances together with conflicting views and opinions. Some of these may be informal and may be settled internally by the supervisor or the Director. In some cases, especially where there are union contracts, there usually is a set procedure to file a written compliant. The procedure gives a predetermined amount of time for response to the grievance, and the next steps as well.

Terms of employment

Each employee is entitled to a written statement of the agreed-upon terms of employment.

Acceptance/Resignation

The employee's acceptance of the job and written notice of resignation are included within the person's personnel file.

Dues

It is appropriate that the library pay the membership dues in professional organizations for employees if funds allow.

Personnel files

A personnel file is primarily the historical and the current documentation of an individual's employment status within the place of employment. To maximize the usefulness of this file, it should contain all pertinent information relating to an employee's position with the library. The following type of information that should be contained within the file: Employee's current address, home phone, beneficiary, person to be notified in case of emergency; application and references; letter of offer of employment; letter of acceptance of terms of employment; contract and date employee began work; written notice of each change in salary. Job reclassification, job title, transfer; performance appraisals; records of commendations, awards and honors; record of acceptance of benefits (insurance, pension); documentation for all extended leaves including military, jury duty; staff development/continuing education documentation; warnings, notices of unsatisfactory work, suspension; record of grievance hearings and appeals; letters of resignation or termination. These records are confidential and only the Director and the personnel officer should have access to this information. *Medical records are filed separately to protect the individual's privacy.*

WORKING WITH PEOPLE

Supervisors are agents of change. However, this does not mean that they miraculously have gained the power to change people's behaviors. No one can do that but the person himself. "People challenges" are probably the most difficult part of any supervisor's job.

When you took on your new job of supervisor, you changed your identity. You now "control" people by gently pushing them in the right direction.

You can now appreciate what it means to be primarily responsible for people rather than tasks. When you had to learn how to do a task, you had to develop the competencies to be able to complete the work. When your charge is to manage people, your job is now to establish interpersonal commitments so that others are performing their jobs. I would hesitate to say that this is a skill that we learned through formal training. How then does one learn to manage people? Part of what we will do as supervisors is what we have seen other managers do in our own experience. I have found that people begin to gather the confidence and interpretations that are necessary for us to be successful gradually. We have to learn to reconcile our experiences with the reality of the job that we have been chosen to do. There will be some trial and error, but through introspection, and from guidance from your supervisor, you will learn to grasp your new role and identify it through action.

As supervisors, we have to learn how to exercise our authority and influence effectively without relying exclusively on the "power of our position." We will need to use persuasion, motivation, and empowerment. Managing people means that we have to establish our own credibility, build commitment among those we supervise, and lead the group. This is how we prove that we deserve their respect and their trust.

There are two types of people decisions that are most difficult to make. These are the ability to be able to balance individual interests with what is best for the library and for the group of people you supervise. The second is disciplinary action of any sort that you must take with the employee. What you decide about problems will have an impact on both your reputation and on your success.

On the Job Q & A

Q: What laws must I consider for interviews?

A: Title VII of the Civil Rights Act (1964) prevents discrimination and protects on the basis of race, color, national origin, gender, or religion.

The Age Discrimination in Employment Act (1967) prohibits discrimination against individuals age 30 and over.

The Immigration Reform & Control Act (1990) prohibits discrimination based on national origin, but requires the employer to obtain verification of the applicant's right to work in the United States.

Americans with Disabilities Act (1990) prohibits discrimination against a qualified individual with a disability, if the individual can perform essential functions of the job with reasonable accommodations.

The Civil Rights Act (1991) allows applicants to seek compensation for willful discrimination on the basis of gender, age, religion.

DISCIPLINE

Every employee should be given a written document that explains what the expectations are for their job performance. In addition, during the orientation process, they should be provided with written materials that cover all of the library's policies, ethical codes, coherence with state and federal laws, etc. Very clear statements that elaborate on what the repercussions will be for breaking any of these policies and laws should be given to the employee at that time. Many libraries ask the employee to sign a statement that they have been provided with the aforesaid materials.

The library should have a written process that is provided to all supervisors about what actions they are expected to implement in the event that the employee is not following these procedures. This is critical so that the employee doesn't then come back and say that the rules were made just "to get back at him." The rules apply to all; the actions taken for not following them must be consistent from employee to employee. Some things may be less serious—perhaps being often tardy for work. Others, such as violent behavior, sexual harassment, and substance abuse, often call for legal action as well as local disciplinary action. As a general rule, you take disciplinary action when an employee's work is substandard or has deteriorated or there has been a violation of a rule or policy. The supervisor must be careful to protect the rights of the individual while disciplining while still protecting the interests of the library.

It is important that all supervisors work according to the system that has been determined for the entire library. One of the very common systems that has been adopted by many libraries is called progressive discipline. Basically, such a system imposes progressively greater measures on an employee whose performance is substandard, or who has failed to follow policies and procedures. This type of system gives the employee fair notice of what conduct will not be tolerated and what consequences will result. Unless the infraction is very serious, the employee is usually given an opportunity to correct the situation. Such a system assists supervisors to be more evenhanded when they are dealing with disciplinary situations. Employees appreciate that this system lets them know in advance what to expect and they have the opportunity to present their side of the case.

The steps of progressive discipline usually include a counseling session with their supervisor on the issue at hand. This session is documented and the supervisor tells the employee what improvement is expected. If the employee disregards the advice, and continues in the unsatisfactory fashion, he or she is then given a verbal warning. This verbal warning is then also documented by the supervisor. A written warning with appropriate evidence of why the warning is being issued is the next step. Failure to improve will then result in a suspension, especially without pay. The final step is termination.

The goal of discipline is not punitive. The goal is to change behavior, enhance productivity, and sometimes both. Employees should be made to feel that the discipline is imposed because we value them and hope to change their behaviors and retain them, not lose them.

Figure 8.1   Sample: Supervisor's Outline on Discipline

---

1. **Assess the situation**

   - What should you do when you realize that an employee may have engaged in conduct that warrants disciplinary action? (poor performance, misconduct, interference with others)

   - Document what happened with pertinent facts (who, what, where, why, how, who saw it, etc.). Who told you? Put this into your supervisor's file.

   - Review the relevant rules and policies. Does it address the type of conduct in question? Has the employee been told the rule?

   - How has similar behavior been addressed in the past?

   - How serious is the alleged violation?

2. **Gather information**

   You should review all information that is about:

   - The alleged incident

   - Employee's disciplinary history

   - If appropriate, talk with witnesses in a private location, one at a time.

3. **Get employee's side of the story**

   - This provides employee with an opportunity to tell you what happened

   - It demonstrates your commitment to being fair

   - It helps you develop a complete and accurate record of what actually happened

   - If an employee is a member of the union, he or she has the right to have a union representative present.

Figure 8.1 Sample: Supervisor's Outline on Discipline (*Continued*)

4. **When there is potential of criminal activity**
   - Call upon personnel director or human resource manager
   - Most of us are not attorneys, and it is important to remember that there are constitutional rights, so get help!

5. **Informal counseling**
   - The purpose of informal counseling is to bring the problem to the employee's attention and to provide constructive guidance on how the problem can be corrected.
   - This step should be taken as soon as the supervisor becomes aware that all is not right. These are some steps to follow for this process:
   - Be prepared, and make sure you have the facts and specific details that you want to discuss.
   - Use a private location.
   - Maintain a positive attitude. Be firm, but remember the purpose is to correct, not to punish.
   - Summarize the conduct/performance, and explain why it falls below expectations and/or violates a rule.
   - Mutually establish a plan for improvement, with a time frame.
   - Recommend training or other resources that are available to help the employee improve.
   - Document the session
   - Followup

6. **Determine appropriate level of discipline**
   The following factors should be considered in evaluating the level of discipline that is warranted by the employee's conduct or performance.
   - How serious was the problem?
   - Disciplinary history? Has the employee had other actions? How recent? Did he or she improve? Is the employee exhibiting a pattern of problematic behavior?
   - What is the overall work record? How long employed? What is the overall quality of work?

Much of the routine conduct of performance problems can be handled at the supervisory level. However, if the incidents involved are serious misconducts, or are potentially criminal, it is always a good idea for the supervisor to go to the Director and the personnel officer for assistance. In additional to the criminal categories, some other examples are: conduct that poses a potential safety, health, or security threat to others; medical issues; discriminatory harassment.

Figure 8.2   Checklist: Conducting a Disciplinary Counseling Interview

- ■ Avoid a significant time lapse from the date of the incident
- ■ Select a time and place that is private and free from interruptions and to avoid embarrassing the employee. Insure confidentiality.
- ■ Review all the facts.
- ■ Have the personnel record on hand at the time of the interview.
- ■ Consider what you know about the employee: personality, work history, particular job requirements.
- ■ Know what you want to happen in the interview
- ■ Start on a cooperative, positive note.
- ■ Help the employee overcome resentment.
- ■ Avoid blaming the employee.
- ■ Stick to the facts.
- ■ Listen to what the employee has to say.
- ■ Use focused questions; avoid "yes" or "no" (closed questions).
- ■ Reiterate and paraphrase statements made by the employee
- ■ Be descriptive and specific about the problem.
- ■ Consider the motive of the employee when giving your feedback.
- ■ Give employees feedback if they request it.
- ■ Discuss your expectations. Point out how the employee is not meeting them, and what the effect is on the library.
- ■ Ask how the employee thinks that he/she can correct the problem, then advise them.
- ■ Give employees strategies to help them meet expectations.
- ■ Give employees a timetable for improvement.

Figure 8.3   Sample: Verbal Warning

Dear (employee)

It has been brought to my attention that you have arrived late for work (specific days and time).

This conduct is not acceptable, and it violates the library's policy regarding working hours and punctuality. I am issuing you this formal verbal warning that further unauthorized violations of the policy will result in disciplinary action.

A notation is being made in your personnel file that you received this verbal warning on

_____.

Sincerely,

Supervisor

Figure 8.4   Sample: Written Warning

Dear (employee),

On (date), you arrived late for work at (time). This was just days after you were verbally warned about tardiness. This action means that you have disregarded the library's policies.

This is a written warning that further violations of the policies regarding work hours and punctuality will result in discipline up to and including your suspension and termination. A copy of this letter is being placed in your personnel file.

Sincerely,

Supervisor

Cc: Library Director
     Personnel Director

Figure 8.5   Checklist: Maintaining Discipline

- Work on an established system that reflects expectations

- Consider the type of offense

- Always get the employee's side of the story

- Show that you are genuinely concerned

- Criticize the work not the person if at all possible

- Identify the issue and provide a plan to help them overcome or improve

- Be fair and equitable

- Keep your temper

- Help the employee maintain his or her dignity

- Remember the employee's rights—union and legal

- Know what help is available for the employee. Make a referral to EAP (Employee Assistance Program that helps the employee deal with personal problems that may be impacting their work performance) if your system has it.

Figure 8.6   Exercise: Dealing With People

The following are some realistic situations that you may face as a supervisor. Think about them, and find a more experienced supervisor to sit and talk about them with you.

A.   You were recently promoted to supervisor of the department in which you have worked for five years. You know that your co-worker, Alice, had hoped to get the promotion. She is a valuable worker and has many friends. It would help if you could have her on your side. What can you do?

B.   It is your first day on the job as a supervisor in a new library. The only information you have about the people you will now supervise is in their personnel records. When you were hired, you were told that there were morale problems. What do you do on your first day?

Figure 8.7   Sample: Employee/Supervisor Session Report Form

This is a sample of a form that a supervisor can use to keep a written record of a session that he or she may have had with an employee. It is not intended to be a "written warning"; rather it is documentation that you as the supervisor recognized a problem, and requested some actions. It should be kept in the employee's file. If the situation is one that was either caused or resulted in medical assistance, then be sure to follow state and federal laws. Most require that medical information *not* be include in personnel records, but filed separately. The most helpful ones are the ones that include specific details.

Employee's Name _____

Position Title _____

Date of Session _____

Supervisor _____

Nature of the Situation/Issue:

Describe it in detail so that there is a clear record of what happened.

_____

_____

_____

Action to be taken:

Describe what actions were requested for the employee to improve performance by what date.

_____

_____

_____

Employee's Signature _____

Supervisor Signature _____

BEHAVIORS THAT ARE WORTHY OF RECOGNITION

We have spent some time in talking about steps to take using corrective behavior. Sometimes we are so involved with this process that we neglect to point out to people the good things that they are doing. It is important to praise when it is deserved, and to be sincere in doing so. If you are very specific and make your praise immediate to the situation, you will find that it has a positive effect not only on the praised employee, but also on co-workers. Here are some behaviors that should be recognized:

- Learning a new skill
- Helping a co-worker
- Giving customers outstanding service
- Assisting a new employee
- Evaluating a problem for a solution
- Being more efficient
- Finding an alternate way to do a task
- Sharing information
- Offering to do an additional task
- Perfect attendance
- Willing to change or adapt

The recognition doesn't have to be costly. It might be a small token, or simply praise, recognition in the staff newsletter, or being named "Employee of the Day, Week, or Month."

On the Job Q & A

Q: My library has different holiday policies for part-timers versus full-timers, and this sometimes breeds resentment. Is there something that I should say or just treat it as the fact of life that it is?

A: I think it is important that the staff understand that it is not up to you but to a governing body to make policy. This may be the Library Board or it may be elected officials, depending upon your situation, or it may even be dictated by negotiated contracts. Communicate the reasons to the staff members. If they feel the policy is not fair, perhaps you could write up a list of reasons why and bring it to the Director who interfaces with the policy makers. The other positive step that you can take is to do something simple that will make the holiday special, such as candy or another small treat for Halloween.

HANDLING COMPLAINTS

Complaints are a part of life. Even the small ones are important to someone, even if you think that they are not a "big deal." As a supervisor, you are a problem solver and it is in the best interests of the library (and yourself!) to address them.

What can you do? Try to anticipate problems. Avoid setting up situations that will trigger complaints. I know that that does not sound easy to do. It will become clear to you if you take the time to put yourself in the employee's place and imagine how a situation seems to him or her. It is important that you listen actively and then act promptly to correct the situation. If the situation is one in which you cannot take an action, then you owe it to employees to tell them why. They may not understand the situation until you do so. And, if the situation requires that you must refer it to others, do so, and let the employee know your action. This will build credibility, and while the employee may still not be happy, he or she will respect you for your actions.

UNION EMPLOYEES

Employment status of employees differs from library to library. Some are employees of the library itself, while others are city or town employees. Academic librarians may be considered part of a faculty, or they may be considered part of the administrative staff.

There are a variety of reasons why unions are more common in libraries than ever before. In the low-paid library world, the most common reason why employees joined unions is because they were dissatisfied with their wages and their benefits. In other cases, the primary reason was concern with job security as library budgets were tightening. The employees have a perception that membership in a union gives them job protection, as they are joined with others—i.e., "strength in numbers."

As with employees, the situation with supervisors is different. When unions are present in the library, it is common that the supervisors will belong to one that is different from the union that serves other employees. However, if all job descriptions with a city are subject to job analysis, with a set number of points given for job responsibilities, it might be that all librarians fall into one bargaining unit and support staff in another. The third scenario is that supervisors are considered management employees and are not in a union at all.

How does this impact the supervisor and the job that he or she does? The most important thing is that supervisors are aware of labor practices in their particular library. The Director has the responsibility of making this clear when the offer of a promotion is made. The supervisor first of all has the responsibility of knowing what is in his or her contract if they have one. Their second responsibility is to know what union covers the positions that they will supervise. Every supervisor has the responsibility of understanding the job descriptions of each employee that he or she supervises. It is also important that the supervisor reviews their contract with the Library Director. This familiarization is important as benefits (especially accrual of vacation, sick, or bereavement time), workweek/hours, etc., may differ from contract to contract. Knowledge of the content will help you avoid a mistake that might cause hard feelings or undermine the trust that you want your employees to have in you.

If you are a supervisor in a unionized organization, you have a dual responsibility. First, you must guide your workers so that they achieve the maximum of their potential. Secondly, as a member of management, the supervisor must be aware of management's commitments to the contract. Failure to follow the agreements could bring about your dismissal and bring great expense to the library. Supervisors should never attempt to influence a labor union; supervisors cannot discriminate against any member of the union; a supervisor cannot retaliate if a worker has brought a change against management. These rules are a result of the Labor and Management Relations Act.

A grievance is a complaint against management. It is beneficial to try to settle this at the supervisory level through an open, cooperative discussion if it is a minor problem. If the problem is a major one, or if it is going to affect a large number of employees, then the grievance should be handled by the Director or a personnel director if possible. You must use your best judgment here. In any case, a supervisor should never try to block the grievance process.

The grievance procedure begins when employees feel that they have reached a roadblock with their supervisor. The union steward is called in to try to reconcile the situation, often with the Director. If it cannot be settled informally, the grievance is then referred to the representative of the local union organization and the personnel director.

The grievance is evaluated at this level, and if it cannot be solved, it is then referred to an arbitrator. To avoid many grievance problems, the supervisor should develop an understanding of the particular contract(s) of the employees they supervise. The supervisor must discuss past practices with the Director so that an understanding of the contract's interpretations are developed. A supervisor can also be proactive in promoting a good working relationship with the union steward and in creating as fair a working environment as possible. Always keep in mind open and fair discussions of problems. Evaluate facts, not hearsay. Investigate the cause of complaints—perhaps you can solve the problem before it becomes a major issue .The best solution to prevent problems is to be proactive and uncover conditions or situations before they escalate into problems.

ALTERNATIVE WORKFORCES

Alternate workforce is the term that is used to describe employment other than full-time employment. There are a variety of circumstances that fall into this category. These include part-time workers, temporary workers, and independent contractors/consultants. Temporary employees usually are there to fill a gap until a permanent employee can be hired. Contracted employees have usually been hired to perform a particular job function, or special project.

There is an increase in these work categories for several reasons. The first reason is that the employer has more control over benefits. While this is usually not good for the employee, it saves management a great deal of money. The second most common reason for these types of employees is because of the increased need of flexibility. This is especially true in libraries that often have to cover a seven-day workweek with no overtime budgets. While it is the Director's responsibility to develop the plan for such staffing, supervisors often must prepare information that can assist the Director in making decisions on the best way to implement an alternative workforce plan. In addition, it is the Director's responsibility to ensure that there is no violation of contractual agreements with labor unions in using these alternate staffing methods.

The additional responsibilities that supervisors under these circumstances include are orientation and training and communications. In order to provide high-quality library services, these employees must all be included in all training opportunities. And, because they may not be at the library at the same time as the supervisor, there must be a very thorough, consistent communications plan in place so that they know what is going on. Another disadvantage is that often temporary workers are in search of regular full-time employment, and have only taken the job with your library as a stopgap. This situation can waste valuable training resources. However, it does usually allow the library to supplement the workforce when needed.

SUPERVISOR LEGAL TRAINING

In addition to the information provided above about the need to know about sexual harassment, there are other specific areas of information that every supervisor must know. These include information on the Civil Rights Laws, which include equal opportunity: the Americans with Disabilities Act which prohibits discrimination on the basis of disability; the Age Discrimination in Employment Act which prohibits discrimination on the basis of age; The Occupational Safety and Health Acts which ensures that employers maintain a safe and healthy workplace; and the Family and Medical Leave Act which provides up to 12 weeks of unpaid leave in connection with an employee's own or family member's serious health condition. Ask if your library or city provides the training, or if you must learn more about the issues on your own. While you are not expected to be a legal expert, you are expected to have an understanding of the intent of these laws, so it is well worth your time to attend appropriate seminars.

9 TAKING CHARGE OF YOUR CAREER

"And all other duties as assigned. . . ." Did you wonder what that last sentence in your new job description meant? It can and should be taken literally, and even though you may not have previous experience with the new duty, look at it as a learning opportunity. The following sections contain a variety of exercises and checklists that are useful in helping the new supervisor complete some of his or her new responsibilities. However, I would not hesitate to ask for direction from *your* supervisor to ensure that you are very clear about what they want.

Figure 9.1   Sample: General Supervisory Duties

You were wondering what your job really is? Here is a list. I know that it is long and can be a little intimidating at first. However, if you look at it from the perspective of breaking the job down into pieces, the tasks do seem much easier to accomplish! Take heart—it really isn't that bad!

A. Helping Workers with Problems
1. Help employees with job adjustment problems
2. Help employees improve performance
3. Help employees find help for personal problems
4. Listening to their concerns
5. Conflict resolution skills

B. Giving Information to Employees
1. Keeping employees informed
2. Conducting effective meetings
3. Responding to employee suggestions

C. Receiving Information from Employees
1. Responding to productivity concerns
2. Encouraging employee participation
3. Consult with them about work procedures and activities

D. Labor-Management Relations
1. Employee rights under agreement/contract
2. Handling employee grievances

Figure 9.1   Sample: General Supervisory Duties (*Continued*)

E. Leadership
1. Role modeling
2. Encourage employees to take responsibility for work
3. Promoting employee cooperation

F. Safety and Health
1. Promoting employee understanding of health services and occupational health hazards
2. Promoting adherence to safety regulations

G. Representing the Library/Director
1. Understand the library's mission and goals
2. Communicate the library's mission and goals
3. Be a positive presence in the community
4. Participate in activities and organizations

H. Employee Development
1. Provide detailed work instruction
2. Introduce change
3. Use teaching and coaching skills
4. Encourage employee skill development

I. Employee Utilization
1. Assessing individual abilities to more effectively assign work
2. Match individuals with the tasks at hand
3. Consider employee interests and feelings about tasks

J. Planning, Scheduling, and Organizing
1. Make sure that tasks are assigned equitably
2. Plan out strategies
3. Help staff set priorities
4. Encourage time management
5. Follow up to ensure work completion

K. Controlling Work Progress
1. Assess daily department developments and progress
2. Monitor individual progress
3. Correct employee work problems
4. Review deadline/goals with employees

Figure 9.1 Sample: General Supervisory Duties (*Continued*)

L. Appraising Performance

 1. Become familiar with established job performance standards
 2. Use incremental appraisal with appropriate feedback for good or bad performance
 3. Remember to use constructive criticism
 4. Document/record so that you are able to do effective annual appraisals

M. Cooperation

 1. Oversee employees in the department as to their cooperation with other departments within the library
 2. Work with other members of the management team in order to resolve problems

N. Resource Utilization

 1. Monitor the resources that you have been assigned
 2. Be accountable for financial resources

O. Administration

 1. Complete paperwork in a timely manner
 2. Be familiar with administrative policies and procedures; keep current
 3. Write reports and maintain records as necessary
 4. Be involved with the recruitment, interviewing, and orientation of new employees

P. Equal Opportunity

 1. Practice equal treatment of all employees at work
 2. Be fair and consistent with the application of all policies and procedures

Q. Disciplinary Actions

 1. Use common sense
 2. Build relationships with employees
 3. Follow procedures: verbal and written warnings, follow up
 4. Have the attitude that retaining experienced employees is a good thing—help them meet library standards

R. Personal

 1. Take the time to understand human behavior
 2. Employ self-analysis to improve effectiveness
 3. Learn how to cope with stress
 4. Remember to give yourself a break

On the Job Q & A

Q: It's late in the afternoon and today I'm all stressed out! What should I do?

A: Imagery is an inexpensive way to take a mini-vacation. Close your eyes and focus on mental pictures from a location or an event in your life that was particularly enjoyable. Try to see where you are. Hear the sounds. Try to remember smells, touch, and taste. In other words, use your five senses!

The work standards approach, a method through which we appraise employees based on a particular set of standards, is frequently used in libraries. This approach involves setting a level of output or accomplishments that ties into the library's goals. Generally, speaking, the work standards should reflect the average output of a typical employee. The major benefit of this approach is that it is based on highly objective factors, so that it is easier for the supervisor to be consistent and fair. The following is a sample list of items that a supervisor oversees. You should see that you have work standards that tie into these. Then you will be able to rate your employees against them.

Figure 9.2   Sample: Supervisory Objectives

1. **Production/Output**
    This is usually expressed as a number of units/transactions completed in a particular time period. In libraries, we normally look at output measures: circulations, materials usage, reference transactions.

2. **Quality**
    This is expressed by the amount of compliments/commendations, or the lack of patron complaints, etc. It may also be the comparison of services with similar libraries, or the comparison of the collection against nationally recommended ones.

3. **Cost**
    Every supervisor in a library is charged with the responsibility of delivering service in the most cost-effective way possible. Is there a better way of completing a task? Does it have to be done at all?

4. **Personnel**
    What is the morale of the staff? Is there willingness to learn new things? Is there a great deal of tardiness or absenteeism?

5. **Safety**
    What are the safety regulations? How are people adhering to them?

On the Job Q & A

Q: How can I avoid stress on the job?

A: One of the best ways to stay in control is to set priorities. Know what activities and issues are important, and deal with these. You cannot do everything—delegate! Remember that the sign of a good manager is not the amount of time spent on the job, but getting the job done.

The supervisor's job is to examine the goals and objectives for the library system. Then they work with their employees to establish specific objectives for their department that will assist the library in meeting its goals. For example, using the safety area from above: *Our objective is to reduce the number of days lost due to injury this year by 5 percent.*

Figure 9.3   Sample: Information Needed for Hiring New Employees

The supervisor has particular information and a set of skills that he or she thinks is important when filling a position. The potential employee also requires certain facts in order to be considered. They are not necessarily different The following is a basic outline that should be helpful to both in thinking through the process.

1. Job responsibilities and authority

2. Critical working relationships

3. Key success factors for the job

4. Key challenges about the job; coping strategies that would deal with these

5. Knowledge, skills and training required for the job

6. Work values

7. Motivation and attitude

8. Flexibility

9. Resources available to do the job

10. Transitional strategies

Figure 9.4   Sample: Supervisor's Guide to Interviews

Sample Questions

The following are some sample questions that can be asked during the interview process in order to get some insight on how a potential employee works.

1. Briefly describe your current position and responsibilities.

2. What does your immediate supervisor expect from you?

3. How is your performance measured/evaluated?

4. What do your co-workers expect of you?

5. To get your job done, I assume that you have to interact with a variety of people? What are your working relationships like?

6. What are the major stresses and challenges of your job?

7. What is the hardest part of your job? The easiest?

8. What, if anything, do you dislike about your job?

9. What do you like best about your job?

10. What rewards are associated with your job?

11. What do you think it takes to be successful and effective at your job?

12. What do you think are the differences between a top-performing employee and an average or below-average employee?

13. Think about the skills, knowledge that you need to be effective as a librarian. How did you acquire them? How can you share them with others?

14. What does attitude have to do with employment?

15. What would you change about the job if you could?

16. Basic background information (review of resume/previous employment)

On the Job Q & A

Q: On occasion, someone I supervise will lose her temper. How can I diffuse the anger?

A: Stay calm! Let the employee vent her feelings. Once she is done, they may be more prepared to listen to another perspective.

Sit if the angry employee is seated, and stand if she is standing. This puts you on eye level and is much better for communication.

Keep your voice calm. This will help the other person lower her voice in most cases. Ask questions, because it is important that you understand why she is angry. Then you can help resolve the problem.

If there is one thing that we all could use more of, it is time. I do not have a magic formula that can add hours onto the standard 24. However, I have found that paying close attention to how time is utilized, especially during the workday, is a good practice. It gives one the opportunity to analyze what one is doing with their time, and to then make the behavioral changes necessary to use that time more effectively. Successful days start with successful plans. You need to set realistic goals and priorities because they are the foundation of having a productive day. There are various methods of keeping track of time. Some people like to use the old standbys of a written calendar or a "day planner." Others prefer the newer electronic resources, such as the Palm Pilot, for this purpose. The method does not matter; the process does. You should investigate the various equipment, software, etc., on the market and select the item with which you are most comfortable.

A daily time log is an essential part of the time management process. It is useful to do this over the course of three or four days. The purpose is to give you a good sense of how you juggle the time that you have during a typical week. Some helpful suggestions are:

Figure 9.5   Sample: Time Management Tools

1. Write daily goals with deadlines as to specific times that these will be accomplished.

2. As you record each item, rank the activities with a #1 if it is an important part of your job, and an * if it was something that was unnecessary. At the end of the day, determine how much of your time was spent on priorities and how much was spent on less important activities.

3. Be very specific. If you note down a block of time just as "phone calls" you may not be able to tell at the end of the day which of the calls helped you move forward in achieving your goal, and which were just time wasters. Note any follow-ups that you will have to do.

4. Record everything. Don't skip daydreaming, socializing, and other interruptions. These are important to the purpose of this activity. You will want to see how much of your time is wasted on "minor" activities.

5. Log your time as you go. Record each activity as the day progresses. (I know that this takes time, but once the analysis is done, it is worth it!)

6. Comment on each action with a view for future improvements. Try to write down suggestions for making these improvements.

7. Do the time log all day long and don't stop and fail to record some activity and try to catch up at the end of the day. You will forget. Remember, you will be doing this for a limited number of days—not permanently!

Figure 9.6 Checklist: Analyzing Your Time Log

After you complete your time log, ask yourself the following questions:

1. At what time each day did you start your most important task? Could you have started sooner? Did anything distract you from completing it? Could you have avoided the distraction? Once distracted, how long did it take you to return to the task at hand?

2. What was the longest period of totally uninterrupted time? What did you accomplish during that time?

3. What was your most productive period? Your least productive period? Why?

4. To what extent did you achieve the main goal that you had for the day?

5. Did you follow your written plan for the day's activities? If not, why not?

6. Were you doing the right job at the right time? Are you using all of the available technology to streamline and simplify tasks?

7. What did you do that you should not have been doing or that could have been done by someone else? Are you doing something out of force of habit, and it really doesn't need to be done?

8. How could you have done what you were doing more effectively? More simply?

9. About the interruptions—were they for tasks that were more important than the one you were already doing? Was it the telephone? Unexpected visitors? Crises? Self? Are you needlessly interrupting others?

10. About communications with others—was it important enough to do? Did it take too long? Are you dealing with the right person? Was your contact inefficient because you lacked notes of earlier discussions? Could a different approach have been more effective: e-mail or fax?

11. How much time was spent on paperwork? Can it be done a different way? Is your desk/office organized so that it is efficient for this purpose?

12. Do you have an effective way to monitor progress on projects?

13. Was time spent waiting for others productive? Could it have been?

14. Did you have to redo any task because haste caused mistakes? Could a task be done faster without affecting its quality?

15. Was the time spent in proportion to the priorities that you set?

There are some other things that you will want to consider as you do the analysis of your time log. You will have to evaluate the tasks as to being a onetime activity, or something that you deal with regularly. Could you do it less often? Can you combine or consolidate some tasks to save time?

Figure 9. 7 Checklist: Tips for Better Time Management

1. Set priorities and follow through in order.

2. Divide tasks into manageable parts and handle each part one at a time.

3. Ask yourself if what you are doing is the best use of your time. If it's not, stop and go on to something else.

4. Select the best time of day for the activity. We each have a more productive time of day; find yours!

5. Keep in mind long-term goals even when you are doing smaller tasks. How are these helping you achieve those larger goals?

6. Streamline or terminate unproductive work habits.

7. Have a list of small tasks that can be done in-between other activities, especially if you have to wait for others to begin those tasks.

8. Insist that you know the purpose of a meeting and its length. Ask for minutes and agendas to be distributed before time so that you (and everyone else) will be prepared to discuss and act.

9. Give up some small details in order to simplify tasks and get significant items done. Make a brief note of where you stopped working on a priority item.

10. Set deadlines for yourself and others.

11. When others do things that either help or hinder your efforts to make good use of your time, share your thoughts with them in a positive constructive manner.

12. Check your communications (written and oral) to see if they are truly understandable, as brief as possible, and to the point. Otherwise, you are wasting your time and someone else's.

13. Recognize the value of relaxing and taking a break. It does make you more productive.

14. Have fun and give yourself some praise for using your time wisely.

Figure 9. 8   Checklist: Tips for Better Time Management and Communications

Communication tools are very efficient ways for us to manage. However, they can also be big time wasters. Here are some guidelines to follow to keep you on track in managing your time.

Telephone:	Use voice mail if you are working on something that a call will interrupt and distract you from. Batch call backs at a particular time or times of day, rather than taking every call as it comes. Obviously, this will not work if you are on a public service desk! But, there are indeed times when having a block of time and no interruptions works well to complete tasks, Use the "Conference Call" feature if more than one person needs to hear the conversation. This actually saves some time over meeting in person.
E-Mail	Unless you are totally dependent on using your e-mail to complete every task, you should also "batch" them together and read and answer them at set times during the day. As efficient as e-mail can be, you can easily see how it can be a huge time waster. Use SPAM software to eliminate unsolicited e-mails. Be efficient when sending them as well. Use the subject line to give the recipient an idea of what your message is about. Be complete yet concise and courteous in your communication. Model this, and others will follow you.
Reading	I know as librarians we all love to read. However, many of us are on information overload and we could not possibly read all that crosses our desks. So learn how to "Power Read." What this means is that you learn how to *scan* materials for keywords. If it is something that is important to your job or interests, you go on to the next step. That is *skimming* it to get an overview of the information. If it seems that the information is something that is going to be useful, you can then proceed to a full *read* of the materials.

Figure 9.9   Exercise: Supervisor's Self-Assessment

The first step in beginning to fulfill your new role as a supervisor is to take stock of yourself. This is useful, because there are qualities and behaviors that you want to model for others in the library. You are not going to be able to do this unless you are aware of your own behavior

The assessment will help you only if you are honest in your responses.

- 4-Usually, to a great extent
- 3-Sometimes, to a moderate extent
- 2-Seldom, to a small extent
- 1-Never, not at all

_____1.   I talk with patrons regularly to discover how to better satisfy their needs.

_____2.   When a patron has a problem, I see that it is solved. If I am not able to solve this myself, I refer to someone who can.

_____3.   I take personal responsibility to see that patrons are satisfied with the library's service.

_____4.   When a policy is making it difficult for satisfy a patron, I question the policy and suggest changes that might be more appropriate for our library.

_____5.   I actively seek out opportunities to speak with the library Director about patron needs and suggestions.

_____6.   I keep abreast of new developments in libraries.

_____7.   I share information that might be important to the library from other sources with my colleagues.

_____8.   I form alliances with my co-supervisors to work toward common library goals.

_____9.   I try to understand the point of view of my colleagues when we are in disagreement.

_____10.   When making decisions, I consider the good of the library as a whole, rather than only the needs of my specific area.

_____11.   I make sure that I communicate information from our department to others within the library, and that those in my department are aware of what is happening in all other parts of the library.

_____12.   I provide help, support, and resources to people in other departments when they request it.

When you have completed the survey, look at the numbers that you have placed in the front space. Are there more 4s, or 1s? Then question yourself what these answers say about your ability to be out in front as a supervisor. This exercise should give you a start in identifying areas in which you may want to improve.

Figure 9.10   Exercise: Getting Started as a Supervisor

These are some questions to ask yourself as you take on your new supervisor role.

1. How does the supervisor that you admire most rate as a leader?

2. How has their leadership encouraged you to complete your work?

3. Which of the qualities that you admire do you want to incorporate into your leadership style?

4. What leadership qualities do you already have?

In the beginning:

1. Make sure that you meet with every person that you will supervise.

2. Review their personnel folder. What training is listed? How is there attendance? Is there a disciplinary record? Are there commendations?

3. Don't try to change everything that they tell you is wrong all at once. You need to spend some time observing, and collecting information. Then you can proceed to make decisions.

4. Identify people who seem to make things work. Review their past projects and the contributions they have made. How can they be encouraged to do more of the same?

5. Even though you have reviewed past records, give each staff member a "fresh start." Ignore rumors and gossip.

6. Hold a staff meeting. You want to see how their interpersonal relations work.

7. Try to decide what they want from you. Review what management wants from your team: reduced costs, more productivity, better quality of work, etc.

8. Set high goals for yourself and for your team. Link individual employees' responsibilities to the library's goals.

9. Fill in the blanks:

   Goals I want to achieve: _____

   Contributions I want to make: _____

   Things I want to help others do:_____

   Qualities I want to be remembered for:_____

10. Be upbeat and positive.

SUPERVISORS AND CUSTOMER SERVICE

Libraries are about matching people and materials. As a supervisor, you will want to be sure you and all who work for you handle customers' requests in a way that motivates them to come back again. The major goal of information services is to make sure that every customer receives the service he or she needs. The supervisor has a responsibility to make sure that every employee knows that they are expected to give good service. You may need to use your coaching skills so that they learn how to provide it, and you must make sure that the resources, training, and ongoing encouragement are in place so that they will be able to provide it automatically. Furthermore, we all need to remember that the goal is to make things better for the customer; sometimes that does make it inconvenient for the staff, but it is our job. An example of this might be working on a beautiful Saturday when it seems that everyone else has off!

Every effective interaction with a patron has three key elements. Be sure that you understand these and pass them on to your employees.

Figure 9.11   Checklist: The Key to Handling Customer Needs

1.   Give them a friendly greeting. A simple "Good morning" will make them feel welcome.

2.   Continue your interaction with the patron in the same friendly manner by using language that is polite and asks questions, rather than commands. An example of what not to do is "Give me your phone number." Instead, "Could I please have your phone number so that I can call you back?" is much more customer-friendly.

3.   End on a friendly note as well. To be sure that the patron is completely satisfied, ask, "Is there anything else that I can help you with?"

DELEGATION

Delegation is an important skill for you to learn as you will soon see that you are often short of time. Delegation is actually a win-win situation in most situations because it frees you from doing a task yourself. This allows you to focus your attention on the more pressing issues. At the same time, it gives employees the opportunity to grow and develop some confidence in him- or herself. So, I would recommend that you do it! However, there are important factors to consider as you begin delegating.

These include the necessity of assigning the work to the appropriate person. This is the person who has the skills necessary to complete the task. Secondly, you will want to get a commitment from the person that they understand what you have asked them to do; that they agree that they are capable of doing it; and that they will complete it in the time that you need it done. You then need to give the employee sufficient authority so that they can do it. Stand by your decision to delegate and let others know that this employee is doing said task at your request. When completed, you will want to talk with the employee and provide feedback. Give them the opportunity to tell you how they think that they did. Point out other ways or methods if you know them.

On the Job Q & A

Q: What if I am the one who is angry?

A: Control it! Take deep breaths, count to ten, and go into a place where you won't see anyone until you calm yourself. Anger and loss of control will make you look overly emotional and unprofessional. If you are angry, say so. Tell the employees that you would like five or ten minutes to calm down. Let them know that you will call them in then to speak with you.

Figure 9.12 Exercise: Create a Delegation Worksheet

Delegation means that you are giving people the authority to make important decisions and the ability to implement these decisions. Your role is:

- To give the staff general information about the task.

- To ask staff to determine specific steps for implementing.

- To encourage people.

Steps that you take are:

- State the new responsibility clearly and make sure that they understand it. Be clear about goals, the expected results, and the time line.

- Ask questions to make sure that the person understands what you have said.

- While you have given the person the objectives, you must give them the freedom to accomplish them in his/her own way.

- Specify the limits—what do you expect the person to decide on their own? What decisions do you need to approve?

- Delegate responsibility gradually. This allows the person to build up his/her confidence and abilities.

- Provide all of the information that the person will need to accomplish the job. If more will come in after the job has been assigned, arrange for that material to come to them directly.

- Monitor their progress. Check on them, but don't hover. Provide appropriate feedback.

On the Job Q & A

Q: How do I know if someone is lying to me?

A: Very often, you can identify lying by people's nonverbal behavior.

Watch to see if they lower their eyes, if their pupils get smaller, if there is no strong eye contact, or if their eyes shift while they are speaking. Watch if they heave their shoulders or sigh. Is there incongruence between what is said and how it is said? If asked a direct question, the reply will often come in a louder, high-pitched tone. Listen for low voices, pained looks, messages/comments repeated several times. Sometimes people who are lying will swallow louder and more obviously. Their faces may be flushed; they may perspire; they may even want to cover their mouths to muffle what they are saying because it is a lie.

E-MAIL

Communicating certainly has been made much easier as well as more timely these days with the use of e-mail. However, you need to be careful how e-mails are worded. In order to be sure that you are getting your message across most effectively follow some simple rules: Include in the header of the e-mail: your name/address; the receiver's e-mail address and the subject of the message. Be sure to be as courteous in the e-mail as you would be in any correspondence. Keep the e-mail to one or at the most two screens. Be complete and accurate. Proofread and double-check all dates, times, locations that may be included in the body of your message.

It is acceptable to use e-mail to write an informal "nice job" type of message, but I would not recommend using it in place of face-to-face communications if you must provide corrective feedback. This might be perceived as not too important, when in fact, it is. Using it as a confirmation that the criticism was delivered is acceptable, but, again, be sure that you have worded your e-mail properly.

The courts have repeatedly ruled that the e-mail that you write belongs to the organization. It is never acceptable to use it with a nasty tone, with off-color jokes, or with anything else that you wouldn't want someone else to see. Keep the tone and the content as professional as all of your other business communications.

LIBRARY CODE OF CONDUCT

As a supervisor, you will be asked to implement whatever policies that the library has. Even though all employees on the front line should and may be empowered to act to implement the rules, most often they will call on the supervisor to enforce them. This is especially true in the area of patron behavior.

Library patrons have the right to receive assistance from the library staff and to use the library and its services without being disturbed by others. Each library patron has a responsibility to behave in a manner that does not violate the rights of others. Their use of the library should not interfere with library services and operations in any way.

Make sure that you familiarize yourself with what is the expected code of behavior in your library. The following are some common rules about unacceptable conduct that is not usually allowed in libraries:

- Talking loudly, making noise, engaging in disruptive behavior that disturbs others
- Food or beverages except in designated areas
- Smoking
- Animals unless to assist a person with disabilities
- Solicitation or sale of items
- Activities (bicycling, skateboarding, etc) that present a safety hazard
- Activities that impede access to the building and its materials (blocking doorways or aisles)
- Use of alcohol or any illegal substance
- The use of abusive or threatening language
- The use of cell phones or other devices (radios, etc.) because the noise disturbs other patrons
- Carrying any weapon into the library unless authorized by law

It is important that you are aware of any local ordinances (loitering, etc.) or state laws (leaving young children unattended—do you notify the Department of Child Welfare) that might also apply. If you are not sure, then it is important that you ask for direction or training on these matters.

SEXUAL HARASSMENT

There are both federal and state laws that define sexual harassment in the workplace. Most organizations will provide formal training for supervisors on this issue so that they will be aware of what behavior is acceptable and what is not under the law. In short, sexual harassment means any "unwelcome sexual advance or request for sexual favor." This is especially true if the behavior seems to be a condition of employment. While any employee can be subject to the harassment, or be the harasser, it is vitally important that all supervisors know the rules. Any conduct that has the purpose of interfering with an individual's work or behavior that creates an intimidating, hostile, or offensive work environment can potentially be classified as sexual harassment.

Some examples of sexual harassment include: unwelcome sexual advances; suggestive or lewd remarks; unwanted hugs, touches, kisses, requests for sexual favors; retaliation for complaining about sexual harassment; derogatory or pornographic posters, cartoons, or drawings. Individuals who engage in acts of sexual harassment may be subject to civil and criminal penalties. Every organization should also have a policy in place that explicitly expresses a zero tolerance for any act of harassment, with disciplinary actions clearly defined.

The law is complicated and difficult to understand unless you have some legal training. The following is provided to summarize it in plain language.

Figure 9.13   Checklist: Guidelines for Supervisors about Sexual Harassment

- Sexual harassment violates both federal and state law.
- The employer is responsible for acts of sexual harassment committed by its employees. The harasser is always liable.
- It is illegal for a supervisor to make sexual advances, or request sexual favors from an employee as part of the employee's job.
- It is sexual harassment for a supervisor to consider an employee's submission to or rejection of sexual advances or requests for sexual favors when making employment decisions regarding that employee.
- Verbal or physical conduct of a sexual nature can also be considered sexual harassment, especially if it interferes with work performance.
- Any verbal or physical conduct of a sexual nature by a supervisor or others constitutes sexual harassment if it creates an intimidating, hostile, or offensive work environment.
- Either a man or a woman may be guilty of sexual harassment.
- Either a man or a woman may be a victim of sexual harassment.
- Sexual harassment can occur between people of the same sex.
- The fact that the supervisor may not consider the conduct to be offensive may not protect the employer if the employee reasonably considers the conduct to be offensive.
- An employer is required by law to take action to eliminate sexual harassment.

Adapted from materials provided by The Permanent Commission on the Status of Women.

SAFETY AND SECURITY

Supervisors are responsible for following and for having their employee follow all applicable safety and security procedures. As a supervisor, it is your responsibility to be alert and report any concerns to the Director before an incident happens. Supervisors must be responsible for reporting all incidents if they involve staff and public. Supervisors must recognize when they can handle the situation themselves, or when they need further assistance. This may be from someone else on the management team, police assistance, or emergency medical assistance. Although not absolutely required, it is very useful for supervisors to have some basic medical training (CPR, first aid) so that they can control a medical emergency until authorities arrive. Additional steps usually must be taken when the injury happens to a staff member. Local policies and procedures regarding work injuries/worker's compensation must be followed carefully.

Figure 9.14   Sample: Report of Work Injury Form

Name of Injured Employee   Date

Job Title   Time of Injury

Location of Accident

Describe the injury

How did the injury occur?

Were there witnesses? If so, list names and contact information.

Were actions were taken to assist employee? (First aid onsite, referred to medical personnel, etc.)

What steps were taken to prevent a similar injury?

Signature of Supervisor_____Date_____

WORKING POSITIVELY WITH NEGATIVE PEOPLE

There are negative people in every workplace. They can make our jobs even more difficult than they are. However, as a supervisor, it is important than you channel their negativity and help them become more productive employees.

Here are some things to consider to help you develop strategies for them.

- Try to find out what is making them negative. Are they intentionally trying to be unreasonable? Or, have they had some disappointments in life that make them always look for the worst? How can you help?
- You cannot change their perspective; they have to do this on their own. Respect their opinion, but explain your perspective using facts to back up your statements.
- Focus on solving problems. Break them down into smaller parts, and then ask your employees to help you find the best way to solve that piece. Things are much more manageable this way.
- Use negativity to your advantage. Since negative people have the advantage of always seeing what could go wrong, they may be able to predict some consequence that you haven't thought about. This can make them feel very appreciated.
- Give employees the room to fail. There are some tasks that can be assigned that if things go wrong won't result in a disaster. In fact, these are good learning experiences. On the other hand, there will be times when they have accomplished what they set out to do. Reward them with praise and public recognition. This helps them develop their self-esteem and can go a long way in developing them into positive employees.

And finally, being a supervisor is a terrific opportunity, but we do know that it can cause stress. Stress is unavoidable; it is a part of everyday life. However, it is important to take control of stress before it takes control of you. As a supervisor, it is also important that you are able to recognize stress-related problems in employees, and work with them to address them. According to the National Institute for Occupational Safety and Health, some of the most common early warning signs of stress are headaches, sleep disturbances, difficulty concentrating, short tempers, and upset stomach. Be on the look for these and take action! There is help available through your local Employee Assistance Program (EAP) if you have one. You can also check *www.cdc.gov/noish* for a booklet and video that are also very useful. Figure 9.15 lists some other suggestions to deal with stress.

Figure 9.15   Checklist: Stress-Relieving Techniques

- Walk around for a brief period

- Plan

- Batch phone calls (use voice mail) and e-mails

- Plan difficult work (reports, etc.) when you feel you will be most productive

- Put situations in perspective

- Prioritize

- Count to ten

- Think of other ways to do things

- Is a situation really a crisis?

- Delegate

- Reward yourself

- Have some items on your desk that remind you of good things to come (photo of an intended vacation spot)

- Close your office door; take a 5-minute imaginative trip

- Learn to say no (This is an important skill. Obviously, you can't shrink your responsibilities, but if there are things that are not part of your job, ask yourself why you are doing them)

HOW PRIORITIES HELP YOU AVOID STRESS

If you do not have clear priorities in your work and in your personal life, you will make yourself be a prime candidate for stress. Priorities are those things which are important in your life; they are your sense of purpose and your direction. Without priorities, day-to-day stability is threatened, and you can become overwhelmed. It helps if you start by evaluating your priorities. Here are some questions that you can ask yourself to do this.

1. What are your long-term career goals?
2. What do you want to accomplish in the next six months or year to reach this career goal? To meet the commitments of your current job?
3. What conflicts, if any, exist between your goals and your routine?
4. Are you finding that you react more to others' needs and demands and constantly put them before your own?
5. How many "roles" do you play during the day? Does any conflict exist among these roles?
6. Do you feel that you manage your time well?

Now, be aware of the distinctions that exist between priorities, deadlines, and job responsibilities. Priorities should be defined in terms of work and career goals. Deadlines relate to particular tasks, and job responsibilities relate to other obligations that you have to your employer. You will also want to follow this same process with your personal goals as well. Then you need to organize each of these categories in the order of importance. Now you have a working plan and you are in control.

If you follow these steps you will find that some of your stress is relieved because you can then simplify the roles that you play; objectively balance important decisions and potential conflicts; evaluate demands on your time objectively and have a good reason to say "no" when they are in conflict with your priorities.

It is also important to remain flexible. Often there are little curves that life throws us all, and if you have attempted to organize your life along very rigid guidelines, you may create a situation that is stressful. Just be prepared to adapt and to accept minor setbacks in life. Then move on and you will get ahead.

Figure 9.16   Checklist: Stress Management Techniques

Here are some basic attitudes that will help you fight against stress.

1. Don't worry about the small things. You have probably heard this advice before and it is not easy to do, but it is important to keep your perspective and not let things get blown out of proportion.

2. Forget about guilt. Guilt is an unproductive, self-destructive source of stress. Learn whatever lesson, apologize if you must, or change your behavior instead. Act don't "stress."

3. Have strategies. You can maintain control during times of crisis or stress if you have reasonable, well thought-out plans that have been made in advance. Whether they are action steps or coping steps, apply them here.

4. Learn to accept change. Take a leadership approach and look for opportunities.

   "Same old. Same old" does no one any good.

5. Change your behavior. Stress is not an external force, or something that is being done to you. Rather, it is the way that you react to people and situations. Change your focus and use your problem-solving skills instead.

6. Develop a support system. Everyone needs at least one person who acts as a sounding board for you. If you verbalize what may be bothering you, you may be able to find some solutions with the assistance of this person.

7. Understand that there will always be some things that you cannot change. It is hard to do because we do want to be in control, but remember that life is a cycle. Things are not always good or bad. Don't allow yourself to be immobilized by stress. Keep busy, change your environment to help.

8. Develop your own favorites as your personal anti-stress program. It can be whatever you want: a do-nothing day; a favorite treat especially if you are on a diet; a new DVD. Experiment and take the time to relax.

9. As a supervisor you will want to remember this: *Don't take it personally.*

   You may find that an employee's negative behavior is directed at you, but it is because you are their supervisor. If you weren't, most times someone else would be the target of their unpleasantness.

10. Believe in you. You can rely on the friend, or the other suggestions above, but when it comes right down to it, you must develop the belief that you can handle it! Give yourself credit for your personal and professional accomplishments and your ability to accept life's ups and downs.